UNAPOLOGETIC:
The (Un)Rule Book

ELIJAH BOTTOMLEY

Disclaimer:

The content of this book is intended for informational and personal growth purposes only. It is not a substitute for professional advice, diagnosis, or treatment. The author makes no guarantees of any specific outcomes and disclaims any liability for decisions readers make based on this material. Always consult a qualified professional for mental, emotional, legal, or financial concerns.

*To the friends who made this book possible by being wise,
wild, unfiltered, and occasionally very bad influences.
You know who you are.*

Contents

INTRODUCTION

What if most of the rules you've been living by were never actually meant for you?

The timelines. The expectations. The weird, unspoken guidelines about what makes someone "successful," "put-together," or "worth listening to." Who made those up? (And why were they so obsessed with hustling, fitting in, and bottling up their feelings?)

The truth is, a lot of the rules we follow aren't real rules at all. They're just patterns—absorbed from family, school, culture, social media. Hand-me-downs we never stopped to question. We didn't choose them, we just inherited them. And at some point, they stopped helping and started suffocating.

So this book? It's not here to help you follow the rules better.

It's here to help you break the ones that don't make sense.

Yes, I know—that already sounds like a contradiction. How can a book with *Rule Book* in the subtitle be about breaking rules? I see the irony. But that's kind of the point. Life is full of contradictions. We want structure, but also freedom. We want to stand out, but also belong. We want to feel grounded—but not stuck. That tension? It's real. And honestly, we don't talk about it enough.

This book lives in that tension—that balance. In the chaos between growth and grace. Between ambition and contentment. Between showing up for others and showing up for yourself. It's not about living perfectly; it's about living truthfully. The kind of truth that can only come from you.

Life doesn't wait for your green light. You'll find yourself emotionally—or literally—stuck, convinced there aren't any good options left. The good news? There are good options, even if you can't see them now, and you don't need anyone else's permission to change directions.

And for what it's worth? Nobody else has it fully figured out either (even if they seem to). I definitely didn't write this because I had life figured out. In fact, I wrote it because I didn't.

A few years ago, during a rough patch, I stumbled across an old notebook buried in a box of forgotten junk. Inside were over 150 made-up rules—ridiculous ones my friends and I had written as kids. Stuff like, "Wrap the N64 controller properly or be exiled," or "If you fart in my room, prepare to get sprayed with air freshener."

At the time, they were just inside jokes. But some of them? They hit different. Little flashes of clarity tucked into the chaos—like my younger self had left breadcrumbs I wasn't supposed to find until I needed them most.

I read through every single one. Laughed. Cringed. Paused. And slowly, I felt something shift. Not in a dramatic, life-altering way—but in that quiet, disorienting way you realize you've been living slightly off-key.

That notebook didn't fix me, but it cracked something open. It reminded me who I was before I started editing myself for everyone else's comfort. And over time, those scribbled-down jokes became something more than inside jokes.

They became this book.

I called it *Unapologetic* because, for most of my life, I wasn't. I was the youngest kid. The "perfect baby." The easy one. The peacekeeper. The good boy who didn't ask for too much. I had good parents (I think), but they often put me on a pedestal, expecting me to be perfect and being surprised in moments when I wasn't. They probably don't see it that way, but the older I got, the more I realized how true that really was.

By the time I was an adult, I had spent years doing things on my own, figuring it out myself, always the hard way. I won't give away too much here (gotta keep you guessing), but patience will reward you greatly.

One thing I will say, those years taught me that you don't get to live fully if you're constantly apologizing for taking up space or asking permission to be yourself.

This book is for anyone who's ever been too much or not enough. Anyone who tried to follow the rules only to realize the rules were never made with them in mind.

It invites you to make a promise to yourself—that you'll ditch the script you were handed, and write one that feels unapologetically *you*.

Inside these pages, you'll find seventeen not-really-rules. Think of them as gut checks. Reframes. Friendly jabs to the ribs. Some will challenge you. Some might make you laugh. And a few might sting in that "okay, fine, I needed that" kind of way.

These chapters aren't linear. They don't always agree with each other. They're a little chaotic—on purpose. Because some days you need rest. Other days? Rebellion. The trick is knowing which one you need and giving yourself permission to choose it.

And yes, I said *permission*. Not from me. Not from your parents. Definitely not from your job. From *yourself*.

Your opinion of your choices is the only one that truly matters.

I don't know what you've been through. I don't know what's ahead. I won't pretend these ideas will magically click or even that you'll agree with everything I say. But if something here loosens the grip of a lie you've been living under, or helps you own your story a little more? That's enough.

Take these ideas and run with them. Remix them. Rip them up. Or ignore them completely and go demolish a pizza while binge-watching something nostalgic. No judgment here. (Well… maybe a little, but it's the affectionate kind.)

Before we dive in, do yourself a favor: grab a blanket, a snack, and something warm in a cute mug. Breathe deep. Settle in.

Let's see where this takes us.

Oh, and one last thing. You've got this.

Probably.

PART 1:
Start With You

If you're going to start anywhere, it might as well be here—with the weird, chaotic, beautiful mess that is you. Because no matter what kind of life you're trying to build, you're the common denominator. You bring you to everything. So if you've been feeling off? Guess what: that's the first place to look.

These next few chapters are about tuning in before you burn out. About learning to trust yourself again, take your joy seriously, and maybe even stop apologizing for wanting more. They're about reconnecting—with your own desires, with the people who matter, with whatever version of peace you've been putting off.

This section covers the good stuff: freedom, intention, connection, laughter, and music. Not in a cheesy self-help way—more like a "remember what makes you feel alive and maybe do more of that" kind of way.

Take a breath. Unclench your jaw. And let's see what happens when you start with *you*.

RULE #1:

Do Whatever You Want

Do you ever try to force yourself to do something just because it's what's "expected" of you? Funny how that almost never leads to happiness. It's like you were handed a script at birth, and the moment you go off-script, people panic. But here's the thing: no one else is living your life. No one else deals with the consequences of your choices. So why waste time trying to contort yourself into something that was never built with you in mind?

The real power shows up when you stop asking for permission. When you say, "Screw it," and do what actually lights you up. So what's stopping you? Opinions from the sidelines? Fear of failing at something new? Let. That. Go. Life's too short to be a background character in someone else's fantasy.

We're so often taught that "doing what you want" is selfish or reckless. Like pleasure has to be earned or justified. But what if the opposite were true? What if desire—raw, honest, messy desire—is the truest emotion you have?

That instinct? It's not weakness. It's a signal. And the fact that you're here, reading this, tells me you're already listening to it.

You ditched the script the moment you opened this book, remember?

I still recall the day my parents showed me my first real taste of freedom. I was twelve or thirteen—peak awkward phase—and life had been a series of rules: be home by sundown, homework before play, bed at nine. But one night over dinner, they said, "We trust you. No more bedtime. You're old enough to decide when you need to sleep."

It wasn't just about bedtime. It was about trust. They were handing me the keys to my own choices. And suddenly, the world felt a little wider. A little more mine.

Of course, I did what any preteen with sudden power would do: abuse it.

That night, I stayed up way too late reading under a blanket with a flashlight, high on rebellion. But by night three? Well, let's just say algebra and exhaustion are a cruel combo. That's when it hit me—freedom isn't the absence of structure. It's choosing the structure for yourself.

That was new. That was different. I wasn't used to having a say. I wasn't used to being trusted with my own boundaries. But when I got that say, something shifted. I started learning how to listen to myself—not just in a moment of indulgence, but in the long game. What do I want now? What will I want tomorrow? And how do I hold both?

Eventually, I realized: it's not about taking advantage of the freedom just to prove a point. Turns out, doing whatever you want means learning to balance short-term impulse with long-term alignment. Sounds like just another restriction— but if you learn to harness that concept, you'll find that it's a gift.

The notion to "do whatever you want" isn't about unleashing your inner anarchist or ghosting everyone who annoys you (been there done that, and it ain't pretty). It's also not a get-out-of-growth-free card. It's an invitation to live authentically—to act with intention, not impulse. Yes, it means ignoring the voices telling you to "stay in your lane," but it also means owning the consequences of your choices and making them anyway.

We're bombarded with expectations from society, family, even our own self-doubt. But life's not a script to follow—it's a story to write. And yes, there are boundaries, laws, responsibilities—but within all of that, you've got room to make a life that actually feels like yours.

Living unapologetically means letting go of the fear of judgment. People-pleasing is exhausting and, frankly, boring. When you show up as yourself—fully, loudly, weirdly—you attract the people who actually get it. The ones who want you, not your curated Instagram feed.

Have you ever seen someone bomb a karaoke night and still look like they were having the time of their life—off-key, out-of-breath, fully unhinged? That's the vibe I'm going for: full-volume, no-apologies, face-hurts-from-laughing kind of living.

And honestly? I didn't get there alone. Over the years, my closest friends have learned how to read me. I can be a little much sometimes—too blunt, overly enthusiastic, weirdly passionate about things like The Legend of Zelda, Apple products, or why every movie deserves to be seen in a theater. I've got opinions. I talk too fast when I'm excited. I will absolutely derail a conversation to discuss the future of electric vehicles or the deeply underrated joy of finishing a thousand-piece puzzle. But they get it. They get me.

Not everyone does. Some people don't know what to do with my humor or my energy. For a long time, that made me want to tone it down—be more digestible. *Shut up, Elijah. Nobody cares Elijah. You're being too much Elijah.* The inner voices of doubt creeped in, and I even started declining social invitations, just to avoid having to fake it or face the judging eyes.

When I finally got sick of the act and changed it up, something amazing happened. The more I let my unfiltered self show up, the more the right people leaned in. The ones who didn't expect me to tone it down just to make them comfortable. The ones who weren't thrown off by my volume or my vulnerability. The ones who could handle the weird and the wonder in equal measure.

There's a quiet magic in being known like that. It's not just about acceptance—it's about safety. When you're surrounded by people who truly see you, the fear of judgment starts to fade. You stop performing. You start being. And that's when the good stuff happens.

Not everything you do has to be performative or perfect. Paint something terrible. Learn to skateboard and fall on the asphalt. Try karaoke and absolutely butcher a ballad. Who cares? Joy doesn't have to prove itself. It's a pulse check—a signal that you're still alive inside.

There's a weird kind of courage in doing things badly, especially when you know other people are watching. There's power in saying, "This matters to me," even when it's awkward or makes no sense on paper. The older I get, the more I believe that some of the most soul-expanding moments happen when we stop auditioning and start living.

But for a long time, I didn't know how to stop. I kept showing up in ways that looked right on the outside but felt hollow underneath. I knew how to play the part—how to be the version of myself that would get the gold star.

One of the moments that really cracked me open came at nineteen, during a my service as a missionary for my church.

At the time, I thought I was doing everything right—saying yes to service, showing up where I was supposed to, living out the version of faith I'd been raised to believe was noble, respectable, and good. After high school, it was the next box to check on the path that was laid out for me.

I packed all the right clothes. Brought my best attitude. Smiled when I was supposed to. Said the right words. Followed the rules. I knew how to present myself like I was exactly where I belonged.

But deep down, I was coming undone.

I remember sitting alone one night, just off to the side of the group, and feeling completely hollow. Like I was watching myself from the outside. Everyone else seemed plugged in—laughing, bonding, emotionally moved—and I just… wasn't. I didn't feel anything. Not awe, not joy, not connection. I felt like a ghost. Like I was haunting my own life.

It wasn't burnout, exactly. It was something colder. Like I had followed every single rule and still ended up feeling miles away from myself. And I couldn't tell anyone, because on the outside, I looked fine. I was functioning. I was pleasant… most of the time.

But the cracks showed. The pressure would build, and I'd snap—lash out over something small, have a panic attack behind closed doors, or break down sobbing in the shower. That was one of the only places I felt truly alone. I'd turn the water up too hot—not because I liked it, but because it masked everything. The sting of the water, the fog on the mirror, the sound of the water running—it all gave me cover. A place to fall apart without being seen.

I wasn't okay. But I was so good at pretending that even I had trouble admitting it.

Letting go of that version of myself wasn't a lightning bolt. It was more like erosion. Quiet and slow. But that moment—sitting in the dark, surrounded by people who saw a version of me

I didn't recognize—was the beginning. The moment I realized I had been confusing approval with purpose. And I couldn't do it anymore.

That's when I understood that doing what you want isn't about being selfish. It's about coming home to yourself. Not in a shiny, "choose joy" kind of way. But in the raw, scary, sometimes-lonely way that requires honesty. And grief. And letting go.

Years later, I still catch myself defaulting to "what sounds respectable" instead of "what feels true." The things we learn as kids are ingrained in us more than we may think. Sometimes I have to pause mid-decision and ask, "Am I doing this because I want to? Or because I think I should?" And honestly, the difference between those two can change everything.

Obviously, not every decision made in the name of "freedom" is automatically wise or meaningful. Sometimes we confuse escape with agency, or boldness with recklessness. There were moments in my life when I told myself I was doing what I wanted, but really I was just trying to get away from discomfort—dodging the work, the truth, the risk of being seen. That's not real freedom. That's just fear wearing a disguise.

I've learned the hard way that clarity makes all the difference—because doing what you want means knowing why you want it.

Doing what you want might look like quitting a job, or staying in one for the benefits. Saying yes to the weird project. Saying no to brunch. Sleeping in. Waking up early. Sending the text.

Deleting the app. Making a mess. Starting over. Let it be fluid. Let it be yours.

These days, I've let myself pivot, evolve, reinvent. Again and again. Because that's the point. Your life isn't a fixed identity—it's a living, breathing draft. Edit it. Rewrite it. Burn the whole thing down if you need to and start over.

And let's not pretend freedom always feels good. Sometimes it's terrifying. Sometimes it's lonely. Sometimes it means walking away from something that looks fine on paper but feels hollow in your gut. Real freedom doesn't always come with a warm, fuzzy feeling. It asks for alignment—and sometimes, that means discomfort is part of the deal.

But freedom without intention? That's just aimless. Real freedom has direction. It means asking yourself, "Does this move me closer to who I want to be?" The goal isn't to rebel—it's to align. Do things that light you up and stretch your abilities, not just distract you.

Sometimes doing what you want means making hard calls—ending relationships, setting boundaries, walking away from the familiar. Self-care isn't always cozy; sometimes it's sharp. But doing the hard thing is still doing the right thing when it's rooted in self-respect and aligns with your vision.

You don't need a ceremonial "go-ahead" or sign from the universe to begin. Start now. Do the weird thing. The boring thing. The thing you swore you'd never try. Whether it's moving to a new city or learning a new skill, do it because you want to. (And if it turns out badly, congratulations—you're now interesting.)

I'll never forget the imaginary kingdoms we created as kids in those overgrown lots. We ruled those patches of dirt like they were empires. No one told us how to play—we made it up as we went. That's autonomy. That's the spark. That's the blueprint. Or rather, the anti-blueprint.

We didn't care how it looked. We didn't care who was watching. We weren't trying to be "good" at it—we just were. That's what I want to find again. That same sense of unfiltered joy and self-trust. The kind that doesn't shrink for approval or soften for comfort.

That kid is still in there. The one who played without a purpose, felt everything fully, and didn't need a reason to be weird or loud or curious. They're not gone. They're just waiting for you to let them back in.

And maybe that's the whole point. We spend so much of adulthood trying to re-learn what was once instinct. And if you're anything like me, you've probably tried to "optimize" that instinct into a productivity hack. But doing what you want doesn't need to be efficient. It just needs to be honest.

Somewhere along the way, we replaced authenticity with performance. We learned to ask, "How does this look?" instead of "How does this feel?" We became masters at packaging ourselves for approval. But approval isn't the same as peace. And applause is not the same as alignment.

Unlearning that mindset takes practice. Sometimes, doing what you want starts with self-acceptance. You are a work in progress—and that's the point. Confidence doesn't come from pretending to be perfect; it comes from showing up, as-is, anyway.

Of course, freedom comes with responsibility. My parents didn't remove my bedtime so I could become a goblin—they did it to see what I'd do with it. Your choices matter. They shape who you become. They echo.

Let me guess—there's a voice in your head right now trying to negotiate with this idea. "What if I'm just being selfish?" That's fine. Question it. You're not wrong for wondering. But also… what if you're not being selfish? What if you're just tired of living by everyone else's standards? What if rest isn't laziness, but resistance? What if joy isn't indulgent, but wise?

What if the real problem isn't selfishness at all—but fear pretending to be something else?

Here's the thing no one really tells you: fear can wear a thousand masks. It'll show up dressed like reason, sounding helpful. It'll whisper things like, "Don't get ahead of yourself," or "That's not practical." And sure, sometimes it's got a point. Other times? Fear is just trying to keep you small and safe. Real freedom asks for more than safety—it asks for truth. And truth, unlike fear, doesn't hold you back. It dares you to act.

Doing what you want isn't always big or loud. Sometimes it's subtle. Like canceling plans. Saying yes to something spontaneous. Choosing to rest even though your to-do list is screaming. Speaking up even though your heart is racing. Those small acts of rebellion matter.

FOMO will have you saying yes to things you don't even like, just so you don't feel left behind. But doing what you want means choosing presence over pressure. You don't have to jump on every invite, every opportunity, every "what if." You just have to be where you are—and actually mean it.

Which brings me to the real question: **What do you want?**

Not what sounds good. Not what looks good on paper. Not what would make your parents proud or your ex jealous. What do you actually want?

That question isn't small. It's foundational. It's a guide. It cuts through the noise if you let it.

The clearer you get about what excites you, fulfills you, challenges you—the more magnetic your life becomes. And the more intentional your choices get. Because now you're not just reacting to what shows up—you're building toward something. Even if you don't have the whole picture yet. Even if the only clarity you have right now is, "Anything but this."

That's a start.

Sometimes clarity begins as a no before it becomes a yes. A quiet refusal before a bold decision. Don't rush it. Pay attention to what lights you up when no one's watching. What makes you feel alive in your bones. What makes time stretch or disappear altogether.

Those aren't distractions. They're direction.

The real win? When your life stops looking like a checklist and starts feeling like you.

You don't need a map. You need a spark. Just go. (And maybe snacks. Bring snacks.)

Because existing is not enough. And freedom? That's just the beginning.

Now do whatever you want. (Just maybe not, like, tax fraud.)

RULE #2:

Live to Thrive

Do you ever feel like you're just going through the motions? Like life is happening around you, but you're not really in it? Survival is easy. Anyone can do it. You sleep, breathe, eat something (probably), and maybe avoid walking into traffic. Sure, that technically checks the boxes. But that's not truly living—that's existing.

Thriving, on the other hand? That takes effort. It's waking up excited for the day, even if nothing 'big' is happening. It's laughing so hard your stomach hurts, discovering something that sets your soul on fire, or feeling completely at peace in a quiet moment. It requires a choice, an intention, a willingness to step beyond the ordinary.

And here's the kicker: if you stay in that gray zone of survival mode, it doesn't just wear you down—it dulls everything.

The world loses its vibrancy. You start moving through days without really feeling them. And over time, the weight of that numbness builds. But thriving? It's still on the table, always. The real question is: are you just getting through the day, or are you actually living?

You know the routine. Wake up. Shower. Scroll. Work. Numb out. Repeat. It's alarmingly easy to fall into autopilot, drifting through the hours like a background character in your own story. And while autopilot might keep you safe—it won't make you happy. Didn't we already talk about doing what you want? If you followed that one, you already stopped asking for permission. Why stop now?

For me, the realization didn't come as some dramatic epiphany—it crept in slowly, during a time when the rest of the world had already slowed down. Specifically, in the early months of the COVID lockdowns, time lost all meaning and survival mode became a lifestyle. Wake, survive, crash out, maybe get a little sleep, repeat. I told myself I was "getting by," but really, I was just existing. (Unhappily, I might add.) I was the king of just-barely-keeping-it-together. Smiling at the right moments, showing up to Zoom calls on time, nodding when I was supposed to—just enough to keep people from asking if I was okay.

But the truth was, I wasn't okay. I was tired. Not just physically tired, but soul tired. The kind of tired that sleep doesn't fix. And the worst part? I didn't even realize how far I'd slipped into survival mode until it became my default.

There was a morning, sometime in the haze of that season, where I opened my laptop and stared at the blinking cursor of a half-finished email for what must've been ten minutes. I wasn't thinking. I wasn't feeling. I was just... blank. That tiny, stupid moment shook me. It was so ordinary, but something about it made the fog lift just long enough for me to see how much of myself I'd muted. How much color I'd drained out of my days. I realized I couldn't remember the last time I felt genuinely excited about anything. Not deeply. Not in my bones.

And then one weekend in late 2020, after months of that low-humming fog, I reached a breaking point. I was lying in bed, phone in hand, numbing out on social media while the sun went down. It was the kind of stillness that doesn't feel peaceful—it feels stuck. I hadn't left the house in a while. I hadn't eaten anything real. My body ached in that way it does when you've been horizontal too long, and your soul aches in that way it does when your life starts to feel like it's happening without you.

For some reason I still don't fully understand, I stood up. Not metaphorically. Just literally stood up. Put on shoes. Walked outside. Didn't even know where I was going, but I needed to interrupt the pattern—even if all I did was feel the cold air on my face.

That tiny moment didn't fix anything. But it broke the spell. And once you break the spell? You start looking for more ways to feel awake—to feel that spark of adrenaline and the clarity of nature.

Eventually, I bought an electric longboard. I had no idea what I was doing. I was half-convinced I'd break a bone in the first five minutes. But something in me wanted to push past the fear, to prove I could still surprise myself.

The first few rides were chaos. I wobbled, nearly ate pavement, and questioned every life choice. But I didn't give up. With time, fear turned into exhilaration. Eventually, I was gliding down the street, wind in my face, feeling more alive than I had in years. That moment didn't fix my life. But it reminded me it was mine.

That's the balance right there: not pushing so hard you crash, not staying so still you disappear. Just moving. Even a little. On purpose.

Thriving doesn't mean you have to quit your job, move to a new city, or become a barefoot digital nomad who lives in Bali and drinks mushrooms for breakfast. Sometimes it just means letting yourself do something weird. Something unnecessary. Something joyful.

Sooner or later, you have to commit. Yes, it's scary. Yes, you'll wipe out a few times. And yes, you'll question why you started. But isn't that better than watching life from the sidelines?

This isn't about glamorizing constant change or endlessly hunting for something new. Thriving doesn't mean throwing away structure or pretending life isn't hard. It just means building a life that feels like something more than maintenance.

And let's be honest—some days, thriving might look like staying in your pajamas until 3 p.m., binge-watching shows you've already seen, and ordering takeout for the third night in a row.

That's okay too. Thriving isn't a productivity contest. It's not some high-vibe, perfect-morning-routine, green-smoothie-every-day performance. It's personal. It shifts. It makes room for humanity.

Routines aren't the enemy. But they should be working for you, not just containing you. Bills still have to be paid. Dishes still don't clean themselves. But that doesn't mean your day has to feel like a beige spreadsheet.

Dance while vacuuming. Narrate your cooking like it's a Food Network audition. Laugh at the absurdity of it all. The secret isn't waiting for something extraordinary—it's realizing the ordinary was never boring to begin with.

One trick I swear by? Celebrate the small wins. Folded the laundry? Victory. Survived a stressful meeting without combusting? Hero. Got out of bed and made your bed? Royalty. These little sparks are fuel. Find them. Make them. Cling to them like your sanity depends on it—because honestly, it kind of does.

Life isn't built on big milestones alone—it's the tiny jolts of joy that keep you moving. You don't need spotless counters, a six-figure side hustle, or a breakfast that looks good on camera to feel fulfilled. Sometimes, it's enough to just be present for the smallest flickers of good.

Also, let's not ignore the power of doing something for no good reason. Once, I bought a bunch of studio recording gear—microphone, interface, headphones, the whole setup—convinced I was going to record myself singing. I got really into it. I watched tutorials. I set everything up like I knew what I was doing. For a moment, I wasn't just surviving—I was creating. Dreaming. Letting myself believe I could be something more than efficient.

Sometimes thriving is letting yourself imagine a version of you that's a little more playful, a little more chaotic—and letting that spark remind you why life is worth living.

Try something new. Not because it'll look good on a résumé or solve your identity crisis, but because curiosity is underrated. And if your brain chimes in with "Shouldn't you be doing something more productive?"—tell it to take a seat. You're allowed to play.

Build a tiny LEGO set and be unnecessarily dramatic in the process. Learn three chords on the ukulele and then immediately forget them. Buy a puzzle. Rearrange your furniture. Cook something without a recipe just to see if you can. The goal isn't to be impressive. The goal is to shake off the numbness and remember what it feels like to be fully here. Not just existing. Not just producing. But alive, in all your weird, unproductive glory.

Not every day has to be epic. Some days, thriving is noticing something new in a place you've been a thousand times. Like spotting Coca-Cola Oreos at the grocery store (yes, they exist). You don't need them. You'll probably regret them. But into the cart they go. Worst case? Weird snack. Best case? New obsession. Either way, you've got a story.

That's where the good stuff happens—in the weird detours, the off-script moments. Try a new route home. Say yes to something silly. Be bad at a hobby. Let it be terrible. Let it be yours.

Thriving doesn't look like Pinterest. It looks like messy desks, half-finished projects, and a calendar full of things that make your heart beat faster. Let go of perfection. Seriously. Let it walk out the door and slam it behind you.

Because thriving is not about doing more—it's about doing what matters. Not what looks good on a planner. Not what earns applause. What actually moves the needle for your soul. And sometimes? What matters is rest.

Thriving isn't just about action; it's about knowing when to slow down so you can actually enjoy the life you're building. Action and ambition are great, but they mean nothing if you're too burned out to appreciate them. We'll talk more about that later—but for now? Just know that sometimes, the best thing you can do for yourself is to pause, breathe, and enjoy a moment of stillness.

You don't have to earn your rest by breaking yourself first. Pause because you deserve to—not because you've hit a wall. Rest isn't wasted time. It's a reboot. A reset. A middle finger to the productivity cult.

Living to thrive is about paying attention to what makes you feel alive. That nap you needed? The book you finally picked back up? The day you said "no thanks" to hustle culture and "yes" to peace? That's it. That's the whole point.

Of course, not every moment is intentional. Some just hit you out of nowhere—the ones where you forget about thriving entirely and just live. Like dancing in the rain. Which for me is in Arizona, where the rain is basically so acidic you can literally taste rainbows. The one time I braved it, my socks got soaked, my jeans were… clinging inappropriately, and I walked back inside smelling like wet concrete. But also? I felt alive.

It reminded me: thriving isn't about being comfortable. It's about letting yourself feel. Even when the feelings are damp and slightly disgusting.

Thriving is noticing the details. Laughing at the dumb joke. Savoring the morning drink. Texting that one person who just gets you. It's about leaning into life—all of it. The mess, the magic, the mundane. Because the small stuff? That's the real stuff.

Thriving also doesn't need to announce itself. It doesn't need a standing ovation or a motivational soundtrack in the background. Some of the most alive I've ever felt didn't come during peak experiences or milestone moments. They came quietly—when I caught myself singing without realizing it, or when I was sitting cross-legged on the floor with takeout, realizing I felt strangely at peace for no grand reason at all.

Those tiny moments, when you intentionally tune out the noise and feel connected to something—even if it's just yourself—matter more than we're often taught to believe.

But the truth is, that's just one version of it. Thriving can take a thousand different forms. For some people, it's hiking mountains. For others, it's finally sending an email they've been avoiding. For some, it's getting through a day without spiraling. For others, it's setting boundaries, or creating art, or calling a friend instead of isolating. Your version doesn't have to be flashy. It just has to be yours. Thriving is just what happens when you actually follow Rule #1.

So. What now?

Maybe nothing big. Maybe something small and deeply personal. Maybe just noticing you're still here, and deciding that's enough for today.

Push one boundary today. Just one. Try a new snack. Break one routine. Say yes to something. Say no to something else. And if you're feeling bold: make it a daily thing. One little rebellion per day. Doesn't have to be dramatic—just enough to make your inner child high-five you from wherever they've been hiding.

Because surviving is the default. But thriving? That's where the magic happens.

So go on. Make waves. Even if it means wet socks—at least you'll feel something.

Let it be weird. Let it be imperfect. Let it be yours.

Because this? This is only the beginning.

RULE #3:

Lead with Love

Without love, everything is worthless. The status. The appearance. The curated opinions and clever comebacks—they all fall flat if love isn't underneath them. And I don't mean the performative kind. I mean real love. Humble, inconvenient, patient love. The kind we preach, but rarely practice when it actually costs us something. The kind that shows up when it's uncomfortable, not just when it's convenient.

Love isn't a footnote—it's the foundation. More than being right. More than success. More than image. Strip everything else away, and if love isn't at the center, none of it means much. That's the truth most of us believe deep down, even if we're still figuring out how to live it.

But let's be real. For something we talk about so much, we're wildly inconsistent at living it. I grew up hearing people say,

"Love one another," only to watch them follow it with judgment, gossip, or self-righteous side-eyes. I've watched people quote Jesus on Sunday and throw people under the bus by Monday. We say "love the sinner, hate the sin," but most of the time, the hate is turned all the way up, and the love barely whispers.

I'm not above it—I've done the same. We preach love, then swerve the second it's inconvenient.

Love isn't optics or reputation management. And it's not conditional. Real love—actual, practiced, inconvenient love—means accepting people even when they disappoint you. It means being kind even when it's uncomfortable. It means respecting someone's choices, even when you don't understand them—unless, of course, we're talking about something criminal (in which case, yes, please call someone).

Leading with love is about being someone people feel safe around. Not because you're perfect, but because your presence signals: "You're okay. You're still loved. You don't have to earn it."

That kind of love isn't always shiny. It's not always efficient. Sometimes it's slow, awkward, or inconvenient. It might look like checking in on someone when they've gone quiet. Sending a dumb meme because you know it'll make them smile. Picking someone up from the airport. Choosing your words with care, even when they're hard to say. Or just sitting next to someone in silence so they don't have to be alone. It's the kind of love that requires balance—being present for others without abandoning yourself in the process.

We often underestimate the power of simple, intentional gestures. A quick "thinking of you" text. Holding the door for someone whose hands are full. Taking a moment to actually listen instead of half-nodding while scrolling on your phone. These tiny acts don't feel like much in the moment, but they're what stick with people. They're proof that love isn't loud—it's consistent.

Say the words—but don't let them become filler. "I love you" shouldn't be tossed around like a reflex or an apology. When we use it out of obligation, it loses its power.

Love is sacred—not because it's rare, but because it's real. It anchors us. It reminds us of who we are and what matters most.

Let that phrase mean something when it leaves your mouth. Say it when you feel it in your chest, not when you're just trying to patch a moment or fill a silence. If we want those words to keep their magic, we have to protect their meaning.

Love isn't a performance—it's a practice. And it's often misunderstood. We're taught to equate politeness with love. But you can be polite and still indifferent. You can say all the right words and never actually show up when it counts. Love isn't about being agreeable. It's about being present. It might look like listening. Or telling the truth kindly. Or saying nothing and just being there.

A while back, I mailed a card to a friend. Nothing huge—just a quick note saying how much I appreciated them. Honestly, I almost didn't send it. I felt silly for even writing a card in the first place. A few days later, they called me, nearly in tears. "You have no idea how much I needed this," they said.

They'd been going through something hard and hadn't told anyone. I didn't know that the card had arrived on a day when they were seriously struggling. I hadn't planned some grand act of support. I just followed a quiet nudge to do something kind.

That's the thing: you rarely do know how much someone needs it. That's why you lead with love anyway. You don't wait until someone earns it. You just give it. Freely, preemptively, even when you feel a little awkward doing it.

Then there's the kind of love that takes actual effort.

I once helped a friend renovate their bedroom. What started as "I'll help you paint" turned into a full-on sanctuary transformation. There were rollers and paint trays and laughter and cursing under our breath when the trim tape betrayed us. At one point we blasted music and danced around the mess like middle schoolers at a sleepover.

I was sore, tired, covered in paint, and mildly at war with their baseboards. But seeing their face when it was done? Worth every second. It wasn't about the renovation. It was about showing up. Saying, "I've got you," with my time and energy. And to be honest, it reminded me how rare it is to both give and receive love like that without strings or hesitation. I've always been quick to volunteer, to pitch in—but letting someone do the same for me? That's where I freeze.

That moment made me realize: love doesn't just show up in service—it shows up in allowing yourself to be served too. And honestly? It reminded me how much I need that kind of love too. The kind that's not afraid to sweat or sacrifice or be a little ridiculous for someone else's joy.

Love shows up. Love pays attention. Love gets its hands dirty.

And sometimes? Love is deeply inconvenient. It's staying up late to talk someone through a hard night when you've got an early morning. It's driving across town in traffic to help someone move a couch you didn't agree to. It's offering forgiveness before you feel ready—or biting your tongue because you know what you want to say won't help. These aren't glamorous moments. You don't get applause. But love isn't about credit. It's about care. The quiet kind that asks nothing in return.

Of course, love doesn't mean being a doormat. Some people are hard to love. Others don't want it. And some? They weaponize it—using your kindness as leverage, twisting your intentions until they no longer look like love at all. And if you've ever been burned like that, you know how tempting it is to build walls tall enough that no one ever gets that close again. But here's the problem with walls: they keep everything out, including the love you actually need. Protection becomes isolation. Safety becomes loneliness. So the work becomes learning to tell the difference—how to stay open without staying vulnerable to harm.

That's where boundaries come in. Boundaries say, "I love you—and I love me, too." They create space for connection without collapse.

There's a difference between boundaries and barriers—and learning that difference is all about balance. Real love includes limits—it has to. I learned this after saying yes to way too much—helping with projects I didn't have time for, always being the one who listened but never getting the same in return. Eventually I realized: I was loving people in a way that left me empty. I thought I was being generous, but really, I was afraid that if I stopped over-functioning, I'd stop being needed. And if I wasn't needed, would I still be loved? That wasn't generosity. That was me trying not to disappear.

Saying no doesn't mean you're selfish. It means you're not faking love—you're living it. Fully. Sustainably.

And yes, it absolutely includes how you treat yourself.

I used to be relentlessly unkind to myself—harsh, critical, constantly measuring myself against who I thought I needed to be. I'd replay mistakes, rehearse shame, and talk to myself in ways I'd never dare speak to someone I loved. But that's the thing: I didn't think I deserved that kind of love. Not from others. Definitely not from myself.

It took time to even notice it, let alone undo it. But one day I caught the thought: If I wouldn't talk to my best friend that way, why was I saying it to myself? That realization didn't fix everything, but it cracked something open. So I started small. Encouraging myself out loud. Celebrating tiny wins. Being gentler. Bit by bit, I started to believe I deserved love—not just from others, but from myself.

You can't give what you refuse to receive. That includes kindness. That includes grace. That includes love.

Let's clear something up while we're here: self-love isn't narcissism. It's not about staring into the mirror whispering affirmations or declaring yourself the main character of everyone's story. It's about not turning on yourself when things get hard. It's about honoring your boundaries, feeding yourself something nourishing, and offering yourself grace when you screw up. Real self-love is quiet and steady. It helps you stand firm without hardening. It softens the way you move through the world because you're not trying to earn your worth anymore. You already know it's yours.

And... yeah. Then there's romantic love. Let's not pretend it doesn't matter. It's real, and it's hard, and it's beautiful, and it can feel maddeningly out of reach.

As someone who's spent a lot of time flying solo, I know the ache. I know the swipe-fatigue. I know how easy it is to feel like everyone else is finding "their person" while you're just perfecting your ability to flirt via emojis. The whole thing can feel like a slow descent into existential dating dread.

Part of the problem? Dating culture barely exists anymore. Gen Z has practically ghosted the whole concept. Flings have replaced relationships, commitment feels like a punchline, and most of us are so used to connecting through screens that even the idea of talking to a stranger in person feels risky—or worse, cringe. The apps are endless, but the actual connection? Not so much. It's like we've been taught to fear vulnerability and chase dopamine. No wonder it all feels impossible.

And that disconnection isn't just cultural—it's personal.

If I'm honest, I still feel a little estranged from the whole idea of romantic love. Not just because of dating culture or the burnout of modern connection—but because of something deeper. Something that started years ago.

I was raised in the church, and it emphasized waiting. Guard your heart. Date in groups. Avoid one-on-one situations that might "lead to temptation." Romantic love was treated as something sacred—but also something you weren't ready for. At least, not until you were older, more mature, more worthy. The message was clear: love was important, but dangerous if mishandled. Definitely not for teenagers. And I was the good kid, remember? The one who followed the rules. The one who took things seriously. So I listened.

The thing is though, I didn't just listen—I absorbed it. I internalized the caution, the restrictions, the fear of getting it wrong. I started to believe that dating was dangerous territory. That putting myself out there was reckless. That if I wanted to be good, I had to wait.

But fear has a way of sticking around—even after the rules are gone.

Even now, there's still a quiet voice in the back of my mind that says, "Be careful. Don't risk it. You're not ready. You're not allowed." And sometimes, when I think about dating, I still feel that old hesitation flare up. The subconscious tug-of-war between wanting to connect and fearing what it might mean.

So I keep my distance. I tell myself I'm fine. That I've got time. That I'm just waiting for the right moment. But deep down, I know part of me still doesn't believe I'm someone people want. That I'm someone people would choose.

Most days, it feels easier not to try at all.

I don't have a perfect answer yet. I'm still learning how to reach past that old hesitation. But what I'm starting to understand is this:

Real love isn't curated. It doesn't live in dating bios or filtered photos. It shows up in the wild—in real moments, face-to-face, where awkwardness and laughter and chemistry get to collide without pretense. That means putting yourself in the room. Letting people in. Creating space for life to surprise you.

Love can't always be summoned on demand. But it can be practiced. And if you've spent years tangled in fear or silence—like I have—it can take time to untangle that. But that's the beauty of practice: it meets you where you are. And when you live in a way that's rooted in love—not desperation, not performance, but presence—you'll be ready when it finally finds you.

Think back to Rule #1: You already chose yourself. You already said, "This life is mine." And Rule #2? You're not just surviving—you're chasing joy. Now Rule #3 steps in with a different question: Who do you want to be inside that life? What kind of presence do you want to bring into the world? How do people feel after they've been around you?

You don't need a grand gesture. You just have to start. Compliment a stranger. Hug your dog like it's the highlight of your week. Text someone you miss. Let love be an everyday verb, not a distant ideal.

And when conflict shows up—and it will—don't confuse loud words with strong conviction. Don't confuse being right with being loving. Sometimes love means taking a breath before you speak. It means choosing repair over pride. It means staying in the conversation even when your ego is begging to slam the door. Love shows up in conflict not by avoiding it, but by softening it. By reminding people they matter more than winning the point.

You never know who needs it. And you never know how deeply it might change you. Love doesn't mean much if you never show it. So show it. Let it be inconvenient, imperfect, human, and real.

Be someone whose love isn't theoretical—it's felt. Be the warmth that lingers. Be the kindness that interrupts someone's spiral. Let your love be bold, but also balanced—rooted in compassion, not exhaustion. Let it stretch you without breaking you. Be the person who leads with love, not because it's trendy, but because it's true.

Because at the end of the day, it's not about what you built, achieved, or proved.

It's about how well you loved.

Legacy isn't carved in stone. It's etched into the way people speak about you when you're not in the room.

At the end of your life, no one's going to care about your résumé font or your follower count. They're going to remember how you made them feel. Whether you were kind when you didn't have to be. Whether you showed up when it was hard. Whether they felt seen, or small, or safe in your presence.

Everything else gets forgotten. Love is what makes you unforgettable.

RULE #4:

Laugh Like You Mean It

Have you ever laughed so hard that your stomach ached, tears streamed down your face, and for a moment, you forgot whatever was weighing you down?

A good laugh does more than just brighten your day—it's a mini-vacation for your soul. Pack light, bring friends, and let yourself get carried away by the kind of joy that only shared absurdity can bring.

Laughter is underrated. We treat it like an add-on, a luxury, a bonus round. But it's not. It's essential. A pressure valve. A reset button. The kind of magic that helps you stay soft in a world that tries to harden you.

And yeah, the science is cool too—laughter lowers stress, boosts your immune system, and helps you tolerate pain better. But honestly? The best part is that it just works. One good laugh can flip the vibe of an entire day.

Life isn't shy about throwing us curveballs—and some of them? Just straight-up awkward. Funny how the moments that make you want to disappear often become the ones you laugh about later. Like the time you tripped over your own feet in front of a crowd, or butchered a word so badly you questioned your entire relationship with the English language. It's easy to let embarrassment take over, but here's the move: laugh first. Claim it. Use it. Laughter turns cringe into legend.

There's something special about the kind of laughter that catches you off guard—the kind that turns an ordinary moment into a memory you'll quote for years. Like the time my friends and I went to see the new Jurassic World movie. We were loudly chatting through the previews, debating the great mysteries of life like it was a TED Talk with popcorn.

One friend had just come back from what must've been a deeply unsettling bathroom experience. He sat down with a dramatic sigh and blurted out, "My butthole is on fire!"—right as the projector cut to total silence for the start of the movie. His words echoed through the theater like an unsolicited public service announcement.

For a second, I wanted to disappear. That wave of secondhand embarrassment hit so hard it felt like I had to apologize on behalf of our entire row.

But then—we laughed. Our whole row. Tears. Wheezing. Full chaos. Even strangers joined in. What could've been a deeply mortifying moment turned into one of my favorite memories.

That's the magic of laughter. It's not just an emotional release—it's a reminder that most of life's messes aren't as catastrophic as they feel in real time.

Laughter is a cheat code for resilience. It takes the sting out of awkwardness, softens heavy days, and reminds us that even in the hard stuff, joy is still an option. It's not just about reacting to what's funny—it's about choosing to stay light when you have every reason to spiral. It's about not letting life steal your spark.

Humor has this sneaky way of turning our most uncomfortable experiences into connection. Sure, we might wish we could disappear in the thick of it, but later? Those are the stories we retell at every gathering—the ones that age into folklore.

The best part? Laughter doesn't need a translation. It's a universal connector. When you're mid-laugh, doubled over, cheeks aching—it doesn't matter where you're from or what you believe. You're human. You're connected.

That's its real power.

Humor bridges things that words can't. It breaks tension, melts awkwardness, and reminds us that, deep down, we all laugh at the same kind of absurd stuff. It's why comedians can unite a room full of strangers—and why one well-timed joke can save a spiraling conversation.

Even the serious people know it. Picture two world leaders mid-negotiation, both stiff as statues—until one of them cracks a joke and suddenly there's breathing room. That laugh doesn't solve everything, but it opens the door. Humor's not just entertainment. Sometimes, it's diplomacy in disguise.

Humor doesn't usually come from scripted jokes or elaborate pranks. Most of the time, it sneaks up on us—in the accidental puns, the weird timing, or the inside jokes that evolve into full-on lore.

Whether someone nails a one-liner or you all lose it over something dumb and inexplicable, those bursts of laughter remind you not to take everything so seriously. They break the pattern. They bring you back.

One of my favorite examples of everyday humor came when I bought a new gaming chair for my office. It had a detachable tray table for my laptop or food. One day, I clipped it on to eat lunch, and my coworkers immediately lost it.

"You look like a grown man in a giant high chair," someone said. And that was it. From then on, it became a full-on running joke: my baby chair. Every time I used it, someone had to chime in.

The teasing never stopped—but it never got old either. It turned a random piece of furniture into a shared bit of joy. I even posed for a photo holding my hydro like a sippy cup, and to this day, it still makes me laugh.

While laughter can transform a mood, sometimes all it takes is a smile. Studies have shown that even a fake one can trick your brain into releasing feel-good chemicals. Basically, your face can hack your feelings.

And smiles? They ripple. Think about the last time someone passed you in the hallway and gave you one of those small, knowing grins—just enough to make you feel human again. No punchline, no backstory. Just a micro-gesture that said, "Hey, you're not invisible."

A smile doesn't fix everything, but it can interrupt the spiral. It can be a pause button. A reset. A moment of lightness with zero strings attached.

You don't need a reason to smile. Sometimes the smile is the reason. Try it. Smile at yourself in the mirror. It might feel weird. It might feel forced. You might feel like a Disney villain trying to pass for normal. But it's a reminder: happiness hasn't left you. It's just been quiet. And maybe—just maybe—it's waiting for you to notice it again.

And let's be clear—I'm not talking about the fake smiling through customer service hell while your soul leaks out your ears kind of smile. Or the kind people expect you to slap on just to make them more comfortable. That's not presence. That's performative people-pleasing with teeth.

Smiling isn't about pretending. It's about noticing a flicker of light—even if it's tiny—and choosing to lean toward it.

Laughter is powerful—but like anything sharp, it can cut both ways. Humor can uplift, connect, and heal, but it can also isolate, dismiss, or do damage when it's careless. A joke only works if the room is laughing with you—not at someone else.

What's hilarious with your closest friends might fall flat—or sting—somewhere else. Great humor doesn't punch down. It pulls people in. It softens tension. It says, "You're in on this too."

Because the best laughs don't come from being clever at someone else's expense. They come from being human, together.

But that kind of laughter doesn't always come easy. I know what it's like to go without it—to forget what it even feels like.

There was a stretch during my mission when I couldn't remember the last time I'd laughed. Like, really laughed. Not the polite chuckle you offer to make a conversation feel normal. Not the tight, practiced smile when someone tells a joke and you know you're supposed to react. I mean the kind of laugh that catches you off guard. The kind that takes over your whole body before your brain can tell it not to.

That kind of laughter had gone completely missing.

Everything felt serious. Heavy. Performative. I woke up each day feeling like I had to prove something—my faith, my strength, my worth. I was exhausted, but I didn't know how to say it. I didn't know I was allowed to say it. So I just kept pushing, showing up with the right answers, doing all the "good kid" things I'd been taught to do.

And when you're living like that—burned out and overextended, always striving, constantly editing yourself—joy becomes the first thing to disappear. You don't even notice it at first. You just get quieter. Smaller. More careful. And then one day, you realize you haven't laughed in weeks.

I don't remember the exact moment it came back—but I remember the feeling. I was with my companion, and we were walking down some cracked, uneven sidewalk in the middle of a brutally hot day, both of us sweaty, tired, and half-mad from knocking on doors that never opened. One of us tripped, or said something dumb—I honestly don't remember the setup. But suddenly, we were both laughing.

Not because it was particularly funny, but because it had to happen. Because if we didn't laugh, we might cry. Or shut down. Or quit. And in that moment, the laugh felt like oxygen. It felt like something inside me unlocking for the first time in months. Like a reminder: Oh right. I'm still in here.

That was the moment I realized laughter wasn't optional for me. It wasn't a luxury or a bonus round. It was survival. It was the way I found myself again—bit by bit, breath by breath, laugh by laugh.

Laughter didn't stop being essential after that. I carried that lesson with me—through every burnout, breakdown, and weird spiral since. And sometimes? It still sneaks up on me exactly when I need it most.

I remember one week where everything felt wrong. Work was chaos. My energy was shot. I was emotionally duct-taped together and pretending it was fine.

Then, right in the middle of the mess, a friend sent me the dumbest meme. No context. Just pure absurdity. And for the first time in days, I laughed—loud, full-body laughter.

It didn't solve anything. But it cracked something open. It let a little light in. Because even when things are heavy, humor has this strange, beautiful way of breaking through. It doesn't erase pain—but it gives you breath when you didn't know you were holding it.

That's the balance laughter offers. It doesn't replace the hard stuff—it just helps you carry it without shutting down. To stay soft in the middle of all the static. To remember there's still something light to hold onto, even if it's just for a second. And sometimes? That second is everything.

Perfection is overrated—and honestly, most great laughs are born from the weird stuff. One of the most underrated skills you can build? Learning to laugh at yourself.

I once sat through an entire work meeting with my hoodie inside out. Didn't notice until I got home. Instead of melting into embarrassment, I snapped a selfie and sent it to the team. They laughed. I laughed. And just like that, it became a running joke.

Self-deprecating humor, when done with care, isn't about tearing yourself down—it's about dropping the act. Letting people see the human underneath.

Laughter spreads fast. One giggle leads to another. One memory sparks a dozen more. It's not just noise—it's connection you can hear.

Here's your homework: don't just seek out laughter—create it. And while you're at it, don't wait for the "perfect" moment to be silly. Make your own reasons.

Find amusement in the smallest things, and you'll never run out of reasons to laugh. Tell a joke. Pull a (truly) harmless prank. Do something ridiculous just for the fun of it. Find a way to make someone else laugh this week, and watch how it lifts both of you up.

You already claimed your right to thrive—laughter is how you keep that promise. Pull up a comedy special. Swap dumb jokes with a friend. Scroll back through the cursed selfies and blurry screenshots on your phone—yes, those. Let yourself laugh, then send one to someone who needs it too.

In the end, laughter is more than just an uncontrollable reaction; it's an acknowledgment of life's absurdity, an embrace of our shared imperfections, and a bridge that connects us all.

It's a form of thriving, too—a way of choosing joy even when it's inconvenient. You've practiced this before. You *know* how.

Look, life's ridiculous. You're ridiculous. We all are. That's kind of the point.

So go ahead—laugh until your stomach hurts, your drink spills, or someone snorts unexpectedly. (Bonus points if it's you.)

Forget the straight face. Life's way too weird for that.

Break the tension. Ruin the silence. Start the giggle chain.

Because laughter isn't just how you cope—it's how you come back to yourself.

And when joy shows up again—no matter how quietly—don't ask if you deserve it. Just let it in.

RULE #5:

Let Music Save You When Nothing Else Can

If you've ever dramatically stared out a car window while playing a sad song on full blast, congratulations, you are a human being with a soul. For the rest of you? Take notes.

Have you ever skipped over 20 songs just looking for the one that will fit your vibe in that exact moment? Same. Music has an almost supernatural ability to make us feel seen, hyped, comforted, or emotionally wrecked in the best way possible. It's like therapy, except it doesn't ask you how your relationship with your parents is going.

Music isn't just background noise; it's a lifeline. It's there when words fail, when emotions are overwhelming, and when silence feels too heavy to bear. It can drag you deeper into heartbreak—or lift you straight out of it. And sometimes, it's the only thing that makes the chaos of life feel just barely survivable.

Often, it finds us before we even know what we need. Thanks to Spotify or Apple Music, my playlists somehow understand my mood better than I do. Sometimes I need a song to hype me up. Other times? I need one to let me wallow dramatically. It's like these apps know exactly what emotional rollercoaster I'm on before I even hit play.

But it's not just convenience. For me, music became personal early. It wasn't just something I played—it was something I turned to, again and again, especially when the emotions ran too deep for words. I didn't know it at the time, but music would carry me through some of the most meaningful moments of my life—including grief. More on that in a sec.

Ever notice how your 'Picked For You' or 'New Music Mix' somehow nails your vibe with terrifying accuracy? It's borderline creepy, but also kind of a blessing. Sometimes, the perfect song finds you at the exact right moment—and suddenly, it's like the universe gets you.

Music helps us stay grounded. It's a reminder that satisfaction isn't always about chasing something new—it can live in those small, personal moments when the perfect song makes everything feel right, even if just for a few minutes.

Think about how entire movements have been fueled by anthems: protest songs that rally crowds, break-up ballads that mend hearts, or that one song that gets you out of bed when your alarm fails. We turn to music in celebrations, in heartbreak, and in moments of uncertainty because sometimes (most of the time), it says what we can't.

Blasting a throwback to remind yourself you're still that person? Listening to a song on repeat because it somehow gets you? Either way, music becomes a companion in ways we don't always recognize.

Some days, it's the only thing standing between you and a full-scale emotional meltdown in the cereal aisle. The right song can instantly shift your mindset—maybe it's a high-energy banger to fake productivity, or a soul-soothing instrumental to stop you from going full rage-mode on a stranger in traffic. And let's be honest, we've all found that one track that nails exactly what we're feeling and then listened to it on loop like it's our personal emotional support anthem.

For a lot of neurodivergent people, including myself, music isn't just helpful—it's an anchor for productivity. It's my secret weapon against procrastination, helping me push through mental roadblocks and get into hyperfocus mode.

Spoiler alert for Rule #8: procrastination is a beast—and music is my go-to brain hack for taming it. The right playlist can turn an overwhelming task into something almost enjoyable—or at least bearable. I use it to push through procrastination and access a state of flow.

When my brain refuses to cooperate, the right music is like hitting a mental reset button. I've found that lyric-free music works best: soft piano, lo-fi, and video game soundtrack covers on YouTube are my go-to. Something about the steady rhythm and lack of distracting words helps me bypass that dreaded brain fog and slip straight into work mode.

As long as no one interrupts me (and sometimes that's the hardest part), I can be insanely efficient and productive. It's basically the closest thing to hacking my own brain.

On top of that, noise cancellation is a lifesaver. The moment I switch my AirPods to noise-canceling mode, everything else fades. The office chatter, the A/C hum, the existential dread—it all melts into the background. Suddenly, I'm in a productivity dome with nothing but my playlist and my to-do list. 10/10. Highly recommend.

That being said, it's not just for work. Music can also shift your mindset anytime your emotions are all over the place. There's nothing quite like blasting an upbeat anthem when you're feeling down or turning to a heartbreak song before the breakup even happens (because you just know it's coming).

Music can be an emotional cheat code, giving you space to feel, process, or completely override your current mood. That's the balance music offers. It doesn't just amplify emotions—it helps you move through them without getting stuck. It can hold space for joy, grief, motivation, and numbness—sometimes in the same playlist. It's not about escaping how you feel; it's about staying in it, without drowning.

Some people meditate. Others journal. And then there's the rest of us, who put on headphones and let a song aggressively fix our lives for three and a half minutes (or hours).

On another note (ha, see what I did there?), it's not just about external sound. Sometimes, music lives in our heads rent-free. And let's be real, it's not always the deep, emotional tracks. Sometimes, it's the most random, ridiculous songs that get stuck on a loop.

You ever wake up with a song from a meme or a childhood TV show playing in your brain for absolutely no reason? Yeah, that's your brain doing its own version of autoplay. Whether it's a childhood jingle, a song you hate but mysteriously know all the lyrics to ("Let It Go" anyone?), or that one piece of a song that haunts your dreams, your mind is literally playing music for itself. That's the power of sound. It sticks, it heals, and occasionally, it annoys the heck out of you.

And beyond what it does in your head? Music can shift the entire mood of a space. A quiet, awkward gathering can instantly feel warmer—less tense—the second someone breaks the silence with a good playlist. People stop feeling like they're interrupting. Conversations loosen. Shoulders drop. Music takes the pressure off by filling the space with something shared, which makes it easier to show up as yourself.

If movies get cinematic scores, why shouldn't your life have one too? That's basically what our hyper-specific playlists are for. "Songs for overthinking my entire existence at 2 AM." "Main character energy while walking." "POV: You're in the final scene of a coming-of-age movie."

A good playlist isn't just music—it's a declaration. A mood board. A vibe. Sometimes a form of emotional damage… expertly curated by Spotify.

We don't just listen to songs. We inhabit them. Ever noticed how you can listen to the same song 12 times in a row because it hits exactly right? That's because music taps into something deeper than logic. It validates emotions we didn't even know needed validating.

Got a new job? Got ghosted by someone you weren't even that into? Just vibing because it's Tuesday? The right song makes it feel like the universe gets you. (And if Rule #1 taught us anything, it's that you're allowed to be dramatic about it.)

Music isn't just something you listen to, it's something that rewires your brain. I learned this firsthand when I joined the men's choir in junior high. My sister convinced me to sign up, and at first, I thought it would be ridiculous. But I quickly came to love it, singing with the other guys, feeling the harmonies lock into place.

Some songs I didn't care for, but others? They felt like soaring through the clouds. I'd get chills when everything clicked together, like the music was more than just sound, it was something bigger than me, something alive. That's when I truly understood how deeply music can move us.

That experience in choir stuck with me, shaping my relationship with music in ways I couldn't have predicted. It showed me that music wasn't just something to listen to, it was something to be a part of, something that could transform a group of individuals into a unified voice. It became more than just sound; it became a way to express, to connect, and to navigate emotions that words alone couldn't touch.

Years later, that understanding deepened when I composed my own choral piece. It was my senior year of high school—after singing in choir since 7th grade—and my grandma had recently passed away. I processed the grief the only way I knew how: through music.

It took months to translate what I felt into something readable on sheet music. But when it was done, my choir director trusted me enough to lead the group and conduct it at our final concert. Hearing my peers sing those words of mourning and hope—for someone they'd never met—nearly brought me to tears.

That moment changed everything. Music wasn't just something I consumed—it became something I created to remember, to heal, and to reach toward something bigger than myself. Just like the songs that carry us through heartbreak or help us push through hard days, writing that piece gave me a way to name something I couldn't say.

In those harmonies, I found a way to hold onto what I'd lost. And in sharing it, I realized: music has the power to connect us all in ways we don't always expect.

And sometimes? Music doesn't just help you feel better. It helps you stay alive. For some people, a song is what got them through the darkest night. A lyric that made them feel less alone. A beat that reminded them their heart was still beating. I know people who made it through depression, anxiety, grief—because of music. When nothing else worked, music did. That's not a metaphor. That's real.

Music is a powerful form of therapy. It embeds itself into your memories and anchors you to moments so vividly, it might as well come with a time machine.

One second you're minding your own business, and the next, a 2013 hit hijacks your soul and you're back in your childhood bedroom, texting your crush on Kik, listening to Royals by Lorde, and wondering why no one told you skinny jeans weren't a good look.

We all have those songs that instantly resurrect forgotten versions of ourselves. The ones that turn nostalgia into a sensory overload in less than four beats. It's why athletes blast high-energy tracks to get pumped, why video game soundtracks are engineered to keep you focused, and why we all have that one song that makes us feel unstoppable.

And honestly? Apple Music Replay is basically a journal I didn't mean to write. (Spotify Wrapped people, I see you too.) You can tell a lot about someone by what they play on repeat. Those annual recaps are emotional time capsules—proof that our taste evolves, even if it takes a few cringey detours. Let's just say my 2010s music taste was... character-building.

Music is more than entertainment—it's emotional fuel, a dopamine dealer, and the only thing that makes doing dishes feel cinematic. It doesn't just help us push through hard days—it levels up the good ones. It's not just about surviving; it's about feeling everything fully. That's the essence of thriving.

It's also the reason we scream emotional breakup songs at karaoke—even when we're aggressively single and mourning nothing but a bad Tuesday.

Music has a way of pulling us through the rough patches. It's a pressure release valve, a vibe reset, and sometimes the only thing standing between you and a full-blown identity crisis over a spilled drink. It turns awkward silences into dance breaks. Lonely nights into solo karaoke sessions. And regular days into scenes worth remembering.

Music doesn't just help us push through—it helps us feel fully. That's not survival. That's how we *thrive.*

In short, music—like laughter—reminds us that even when life is in disarray, there's still joy to be found in the insanity. It's the friend that hypes you up, comforts you, and sometimes drags you into feelings you didn't ask for but probably needed.

So, blast that song. Let it level you. Let it lift you. Let it become the soundtrack to your healing.

Music won't fix everything—but it'll ride shotgun, sing the chorus, and remind you that you're still here.

Let music save you when nothing else can.

Press play. Cry dramatically. Repeat as needed.

PART 2:
Get Real

Alright, so you've started showing up. You're doing the thing. You're being bold, being weird, maybe even crying in your car to a sad song that hits too hard. You're letting yourself feel again—and honestly? That's huge.

But here's what no one tells you: once you start living more honestly, things get louder.

You'll feel confident one minute, then suddenly spiral over a text you sent four hours ago. You'll be vibing, then procrastinate for six days straight and wonder if you're actually a total fraud. That inner critic? Louder than ever. And your old patterns? Oh, they love a comeback tour.

This section is where we deal with all of that.

It's about calling yourself in—before your brain hijacks your week. About being honest, not just performative. About making decisions that actually line up with your values instead of your anxiety. And yeah, it's about holding your own hand through the cringe.

These next few rules? They're less "manifest your dream life" and more "sit down, take a breath, and be honest with yourself."

Because getting real isn't about having it all figured out.

It's about refusing to pretend anymore.

Deep breath. We're going in.

RULE #6:

Judge with Kindness

We usually think of judgment as something we aim outward—at other people, their choices, their weird condiment habits. But the harshest judgment often lives inside our own heads. This chapter is about both. The voice that shames you when you screw up, and the quick assumptions we make about others when we don't have the full story. Either way, kindness is the antidote.

We all have that voice in our heads. You know the one. It pipes up the moment you misstep, magnifying small mistakes into catastrophic failures. Spill your drink on your shirt? Great job, genius. Forget to respond to an email? Way to ruin your reputation. It's like having your own personal critic living rent-free in your brain, and no matter how many times you try to evict it, it just keeps coming back.

And not just toward yourself—recognizing this inner critic is the first step toward learning how to judge with kindness—toward others and yourself. It's not about silencing that voice entirely, it's about realizing that it doesn't always deserve the microphone. Just because your brain decides to narrate your life like an apocalypse movie doesn't mean you have to buy into every plot twist.

Take the time I forgot to pay my car payment. For a solid day, I convinced myself this was the beginning of my financial downfall. I envisioned late fees spiraling out of control, my credit score tanking, and some stern stranger on the phone lecturing me about responsibility.

Finally, I called the company. The whole thing was resolved in two minutes—no fees, no lecture, no drama. The world hadn't ended. Shocking, right?

That kind of overreaction isn't unique to me—it's human. We all let our inner critic take the wheel sometimes, steering us straight into self-condemnation. But self-blame doesn't fix the mistake. It just makes the ride bumpier.

Offering yourself compassion in those moments is like pulling over to patch the tire—not slashing until it's beyond saving. Compassion doesn't erase the mistake. It just changes how you carry it.

Self-awareness is a game-changer. Start by paying attention to the voice in your head for the next few days. Notice its tone, its patterns, and how it makes you feel. Does it exaggerate your mistakes? Does it downplay your wins?

That inner critic is loud—but rarely accurate. It fixates on what went wrong and glosses over what's going right. Think about how often you've brushed off a compliment but obsessed over a tiny critique for hours. That imbalance messes with your perception, turning small setbacks into catastrophes while making your wins feel forgettable.

But once you see the voice for what it is—not truth, just your internal narrator talking like it knows the whole story—it gets easier to roll your eyes and keep moving before it hijacks your whole day.

Judging yourself harshly doesn't just rob you of joy—it locks you into patterns of fear and hesitation. Because how you treat yourself—the tone you set in your own head—inevitably spills outward. You're not just practicing judgment. You're rehearsing how to aim it at other people, too.

Remember Rule #1 and its call to take ownership of your freedom? Part of that means giving yourself room to be imperfect. Freedom isn't about never messing up—it's about having permission to keep going anyway.

And honestly? You probably will mess up again. Maybe a lot. That's not failure—that's movement. Every awkward attempt is still forward motion if you're paying attention. Progress isn't about flawless execution. It's about showing up, again and again, even when you don't quite stick the landing.

Of course, being kind to yourself doesn't mean dodging responsibility. If you miss a deadline, beating yourself up won't fix it—but pretending it didn't happen won't help either. The move isn't shame or denial. It's: yeah, that sucked—now what?

That's the balance: take it seriously, without internalizing and turning it into a character assassination. You made a mistake. Cool, so does everyone. You still deserve the same grace you'd give a friend.

There's a big difference between "I messed up, so I must be a disaster," and "I messed up. Here's how I'll handle it next time."

Accountability without kindness? That's just punishment. But kindness without accountability? That's comfort with no growth. Real growth lives somewhere in between.

The world doesn't respond to self-pity or denial—it responds to honesty. Because honesty signals that you're self-aware enough to grow, not just perform. It shows people you're paying attention. That you're in the work, not hiding from it. When you meet your mistakes with honesty and grace, you can learn from them without letting them define you. Missteps aren't detours from growth; they're how you get there.

And here's the twist: owning your mess often earns more respect than hiding it. I once missed a deadline at work and instead of scrambling for an excuse, I just said, 'Yeah, that one's on me. I'll fix it.' I braced for the awkward sigh or some mini-lecture—but my manager just nodded and thanked me for being honest. That was it. No drama. No weird tension. Vulnerability in those moments has a way of softening judgment—your own, and everyone else's.

We don't just judge ourselves—we judge other people, too. Sometimes it's harsh, but sometimes? It's just part of the bit.

There was a stretch at work where I felt like no matter what I did, someone had something to say. I got written up for being late a few too many times. And sure, I knew I was cutting it close—but I also knew why. I'd tried to explain it to my manager: things at home weren't easy. Mornings were unpredictable. Living with mentally unstable family members meant I didn't always know if the bathroom would be free, or if I'd be stuck navigating chaos before I even got out the door.

I was honest. Vulnerable, even. But they didn't want the nuance. They wanted punctuality. They wrote it off as excuses and moved on.

That kind of judgment sticks. Not just because it's unfair, but because it makes you start questioning yourself. You start wondering if maybe they're right. If maybe you're not trying hard enough, even when you know how hard you are.

And it wasn't just that. People started reporting that I was "always on my phone"—even though it was literally during my scheduled breaks. So I stopped taking breaks at my desk. Started eating lunch in my car. Not for peace and quiet—just to avoid being misunderstood.

What got to me wasn't just the judgment—it was how fast I started shaping my behavior around it. Not because I was doing anything wrong, but because I didn't want to give anyone more ammo to misread me. That's the thing about judgment:

it doesn't just notice—it assumes. Kindness? It pauses. It asks. And sometimes, that pause is the difference between feeling seen and feeling like you have to disappear.

Eventually, I hit a wall. Not some big dramatic moment—just a quiet shift. I stopped trying to explain myself to people who didn't actually want to understand. I realized I was spending more energy managing perception than just living my life. So I backed off. I kept showing up. Kept doing my job. But I stopped carrying the pressure to make everyone else comfortable with how I exist.

That was a turning point. Because judgment—especially the silent, side-eye kind—can train you to shrink. And unlearning that? That's where the real work is.

Most judgment doesn't come from malice—it comes from not knowing the whole story. And the truth is, we rarely do. That's why I've tried to lead with curiosity, both with others and with myself. Because when you've been on the receiving end of judgment that misses the mark, you learn just how much damage a snap assumption can do.

Like the time my friends and I were at Sonic, and one of my buddies squirted an entire ketchup packet all over his vanilla ice cream cone. We all stared in horror, exchanging glances like, *Is he serious?*—before bursting into laughter.

We judged him, obviously. But it was the kind that comes with raised eyebrows and inside jokes, not ridicule. Because some choices do deserve a little roasting—*as long as it's done with care.*

And in the grand scheme of things, wouldn't it be better if more of our judgments felt like that? Like inside jokes, not harsh verdicts?

Here's a radical thought you've definitely never heard before: what if you treated others with the same generosity you're learning to offer yourself?

We've all misjudged someone before, only to realize later that we didn't have the full story. I remember getting frustrated with a friend who canceled plans last minute—I assumed they just didn't care. Turns out, they were dealing with a family emergency they hadn't told anyone about.

And the second I found out, I felt that quiet kind of regret—the kind that doesn't announce itself, just lingers. Not because they made me feel guilty, but because I realized how quickly I'd filled in the blanks with the wrong story. That moment stuck with me. How often do we judge before we understand?

People aren't perfect, and acting surprised every time someone slips up is exhausting—for you *and* them. Recognizing that everyone's a work in progress doesn't mean excusing bad behavior, but it does create space for empathy.

Think about a time you were forgiven for something you didn't handle well. That sense of relief—knowing someone saw your intentions instead of just your actions—is powerful. Why not offer that same relief to others?

Grace extended outward has a way of multiplying. It creates a ripple effect, turning a single moment of grace into a chain of positive interactions.

Forgiveness is one of the most misunderstood acts of strength. It's not passive, and it's not naive. It doesn't mean you condone what happened—or that you forget it. It doesn't mean pretending it didn't hurt. It just means you're choosing to stop being the one carrying the weight of it. Sometimes, forgiveness is simply loosening your grip so you can finally exhale. That's not weakness—it's choosing peace over bitterness. And some days, that choice is everything.

Judgment holds people in the past. Forgiveness frees them to move forward—even if you never speak again. And sometimes, it's not about healing the relationship. It's about healing yourself from the pain that came with it.

Some people may never apologize. They may never change. And still, forgiveness can be yours. Because it's not something they earn—it's something you choose. Mercy isn't weakness—it's a widening of your spirit. It says: *this doesn't get to harden me. This doesn't get to shrink me.*

Some people don't deserve your forgiveness. But you do. Not for their sake—for your peace. Your freedom. Your future.

Judging with clarity and care isn't just about being nice—it's about creating a world where growth is actually possible.

Harsh judgment, whether aimed at yourself or others, builds walls. Compassion builds bridges. When you judge fairly, you make space for progress instead of perfection—and that's a game worth playing.

By choosing compassion over condemnation, you invite yourself (and everyone around you) to show up imperfect and still try anyway. It's not always easy—but it's always worth it.

Kindness isn't weakness. It's clarity. It's strength. And maybe next time your inner critic starts ranting, you'll roll your eyes, laugh a little, and keep writing the story you actually want to live.

Because this isn't about lowering your standards. It's about elevating your perspective.

No one is keeping score of your worst moments—except maybe you. And let's be real, you're a pretty unreliable narrator. Life isn't a courtroom where every mistake is on trial. If it were, we'd all be guilty of something ridiculous. Like that one time you confidently waved back at someone who wasn't actually waving at you. (Ouch.)

Life is a rollercoaster that you're building while riding, and the only real failure is refusing to move forward. Take a breath. Offer kindness. See the bigger picture. Give people the benefit of the doubt.

And for the love of all things good, stop expecting perfection from imperfect people. If you absolutely must judge someone, at least be creative about it. Like asking nicely why they put ketchup on ice cream instead of assuming they're a total weirdo. Curiosity: good. Condescension: not so much. Unless they're putting mustard on it too—then we riot.

The next time your inner critic or snap judgment kicks in, pause before you hand it the mic. Call it out. Question it. Remind yourself: not every thought deserves your belief.

Would you talk to your best friend like that? No? Then don't talk to yourself that way either.

Kindness isn't letting yourself off the hook. It's choosing to heal instead of harm. To learn instead of spiral.

And if you absolutely have to judge someone? Do it with a little creativity, a lot of empathy, and maybe a side of Sonic ketchup.

The more I practice judging with kindness, the better I get at seeing people clearly—including myself.

Because when you lead with love instead of criticism—even with yourself—you don't just make life lighter.

You make it *yours*.

RULE #7:

Commit to Honesty

Let's be honest about honesty: it's not always soft and noble. Sometimes it's awkward. Sometimes it's loud. Sometimes it shows up uninvited and ruins your whole vibe. But whether it's a quiet truth you've been dodging or something big you need to say out loud, the same rule applies—it matters. This chapter is about both kinds of honesty: the stuff you owe to other people, and the stuff you can't keep avoiding with yourself. Because when you keep dodging the truth, life starts to feel fake. And you do too.

Everyone lies. Sometimes it's a "Yeah, I'm on my way" text when you haven't even left the house. Other times, it's telling yourself you're "fine" when you're absolutely not. The problem isn't just the lies themselves—it's how they chip away at trust, authenticity, and eventually, your peace of mind.

Honesty isn't just about being truthful with others; it's the foundation of self-respect and real connection. The more you compromise it, the shakier everything else gets.

We all sidestep the truth sometimes—to avoid conflict, to make things easier, or to protect our egos. It's scary to admit you messed up. To tell a friend something they might not want to hear. To face a truth about yourself you've been trying to ignore.

But dodging reality doesn't make the problem disappear. It just pushes it further down the road—usually into a bigger mess.

Imagine honesty as the framework of a sturdy house. Every time you avoid telling the truth—whether to yourself or someone else—it's like replacing a solid wooden beam with cheap, hollow drywall. At first, the structure still stands, but over time, as more and more weak materials are used, it becomes unstable. One day, a storm hits, and the entire thing collapses—not because of one flaw, but because of all the little cracks that added up.

That's what dishonesty does to your life. Little lies may feel harmless in the moment: shrugging off how you really feel, pretending something doesn't bother you, or making excuses for why you're not pursuing what you actually want. But those moments accumulate. Every time you lie to yourself, even a little, you teach your brain not to believe you. And one day, you look around and realize you've built a life on shaky ground—a version of yourself that doesn't quite feel real.

I once got upset with a friend over something they said. Nothing explosive—just one of those quiet little comments that lands sideways and sticks. But instead of saying anything, I hit them with a classic "It's fine" and tried to swallow the feeling like it was no big deal. Spoiler: it was a big deal. And my body language? Probably louder than I realized.

A few days later, they circled back. "Hey, I feel like something's off. Did I do something?" And that's when it all came out. I finally admitted what had rubbed me the wrong way, and they listened. They even apologized. But I could tell they were hurt—not because I was upset, but because I hadn't trusted them enough to be real about it from the start.

That moment stuck with me. I thought I was keeping the peace by brushing it off. But really, I was just delaying the discomfort. And in doing that, I made it worse.

That small lie chipped away at our trust. It didn't feel like a big deal in the moment, but even tiny deceptions have a way of adding up. Over time, they create cracks—not just in your relationships, but in your sense of who you are.

Let's get one thing straight: honesty and cruelty are not the same thing. Saying, "Your haircut looks like a lawnmower attack" might be honest-ish, but it doesn't make you a truth-teller—it makes you kind of a jerk.

Real honesty is rooted in clarity and care. It's not about steamrolling someone's insecurities just in the name of truth.

I learned that the hard way when I asked a close friend for feedback on something I'd poured my heart into. I'd been working on this thing for weeks—tweaking every word, second-guessing every choice, trying to create something that actually felt like me. By the time I sent it over, I was proud… and also terrified. That combo platter of "I love this" and "Please don't hate it" was doing laps in my chest.

Their response? A rapid-fire list of everything they thought I should change. Not a "Hey, I see what you're going for," or a "This part really works." Just edits. Corrections. Red ink everywhere. They weren't trying to be hurtful—they thought they were being helpful. But it still landed like a punch.

And the part that surprised me most? I wasn't just hurt by what they said—I was hurt by how quickly they skipped past what it meant to me. I didn't need ego-stroking. But I did need them to see the effort. The risk. The part of me that was embedded in the thing.

That moment stuck with me. It reminded me that honesty isn't just about being real—it's about being responsible with how blunt you are.

Because truth, when delivered without empathy, can feel a lot like rejection. And if we want our honesty to land—to actually make a difference instead of just making noise—we've got to wrap it in care.

Which brings me to the key question: how can you tell the truth without hurting people?

Well, first of all, don't weaponize it. Timing matters. Delivery matters. Blurting out your hot take in the middle of an argument doesn't make you honest—it makes you reckless. The truth is more likely to land when the moment feels safe, not when emotions are already high and everyone is one comment away from turning into a reality show meltdown.

Being honest isn't just about saying what's real—it's about saying it well. That means choosing your words carefully, understanding the context, and asking yourself whether what you're about to say will actually help the person grow—or just make them feel small.

Truth isn't less true when it's delivered with care. If anything, that's when it actually becomes useful.

That's the thing about honesty—it's not just about how you talk to others. It's also about how you talk to *yourself.* And let's be real: that's often the hardest truth to face. There's no hiding from your own reflection, but that doesn't stop us from trying. We downplay our fears, inflate our confidence, and insist we're "fine" when everything inside us says otherwise.

Looking back, I can see how long I tried to convince myself I was happy following a path that never really felt like mine. You've already heard parts of the mission story—but this is the truth I didn't know how to name at the time.

I kept telling myself I was where I was meant to be. That I just needed to push through. That the pit in my stomach was something to pray away, not pay attention to.

Meanwhile, I watched others around me break the rules left and right—sneaking out, lying to leadership, bending the boundaries without a second thought. I saw more deception in that year than I'd seen in my entire life, including from the leadership themselves, and I started to feel like I was part of some elaborate show. Like we were all just performers, selling something we didn't fully believe. And me? I was the good one. The honest one. The one who followed the rules.

Until I couldn't anymore.

When I finally admitted I wanted to go home, people told me I was turning my back on God. That I lacked faith. That I would be "*thrust down to hell*"—actual words from a leader. But I knew myself better than they did. I knew I was unraveling. My anxiety had reached a point where I was snapping at people, crying without knowing why, floating outside my own body like I was watching someone else live my life. I didn't feel lost. I felt erased.

I remember the exact moment I decided to leave. After months of praying for a sign or a reason to stay, I realized I wasn't actually looking for answers—I was looking for permission. That shift changed everything.

This isn't me saying the church or all of the people in it were liars. I'm also not saying that the entire experience was terrible. But I was lying to myself about wanting to be there with those people.

Once I told the truth—the full, unfiltered truth—to my parents and senior church leadership, I felt the weight lift. Not completely, and not overnight. But for the first time in a long time, I could breathe. I could move forward.

I may never fully understand why I went on that mission, or what became of the people I left behind. But I do know this:

telling the truth was the right call. For them, maybe—but for me, definitely. That moment taught me something I still come back to when things get hard: honesty doesn't always fix everything, but it clears the fog. It helps you see the road again.

Once you see clearly, it gets harder to keep looking away.

Have you ever realized you weren't pursuing the things that truly made you happy? Maybe it was easier to stick with the status quo than to face the upheaval of change. Perhaps you buried that nagging feeling, told yourself it wasn't so bad, or rationalized the situation with excuses. But ignoring that inner truth doesn't make it go away—it just delays the reckoning. Those whispers of dissatisfaction only grow louder over time, demanding your attention.

Being honest with yourself might feel like peeling back a bandage, but it's the only way to repair those cracks.

Telling the truth—especially to yourself—isn't just about growth. It's about getting unstuck. It's how you stop spinning in circles and start actually moving forward.

And when you do? Things shift. You stop faking it. You start choosing—what to care about, who to trust, how to show up. You stop living on autopilot and start building a life that actually feels like yours. Even the hard days hit different, because at least you're the one driving.

When you're living in truth, you stop wasting energy on managing impressions or dodging discomfort. You set boundaries with less guilt, and you start building deeper relationships—not by oversharing or forcing connection, but by telling the truth when it counts.

So, next time you catch yourself saying "It's fine" or "I'll deal with it later," pause. Ask yourself what you're really avoiding. Honesty might not give you an easy way out, but it will give you clarity and the courage to move forward with intention. And the more you practice it, the easier it becomes. Choosing honesty repeatedly will make it your natural instinct rather than an uncomfortable obligation.

Dishonesty doesn't just erode relationships—it erodes you. Every time you suppress what you really feel, you chip away at your own identity. You start living someone else's version of your life. One that's quieter, safer, but *smaller.* One built not on who you are, but on who you think you're supposed to be.

Shortcuts are tempting: fudging a résumé, telling a "small" lie to avoid conflict, or pretending you're okay when you're not. But white lies that compromise your integrity often come with long-term costs. Half-truths and suppressed emotions accumulate like clutter in an overstuffed drawer. At first, they seem manageable, but eventually, they overflow and create a disaster that's impossible to ignore.

Addressing things honestly, even when it's uncomfortable, is like cleaning out that drawer: tedious, sometimes a little painful, but always worth it. It clears space—not just in your closet, but in your mind and spirit.

When you embrace honesty, you create an environment where trust can flourish. Openness takes courage. It's standing in the middle of emotional turmoil and saying, "Let's clean this up together."

Honesty isn't about accusing; it's about inviting understanding. It's the glue that holds meaningful relationships together, the compass that keeps you aligned with your values, and the foundation that ensures you're living life on your terms.

And if Rule #6 taught us anything, it's that judgment might build walls—but truth, when paired with compassion, can still build bridges.

Here's the hard truth: honesty isn't just about not breaking trust—it's about repairing it when it's already shattered. And that part? That's not easy. If you've ever lied to someone you care about—whether by omission, avoidance, or outright deception—you know that no amount of "I'm sorry" can instantly undo the damage. Trust is like glass: when it breaks, you can piece it back together, but it'll never look exactly the same. That's the bad news.

The good news? It can still be strong. Maybe even stronger than before. But only if you commit to showing up with honesty—not once, but over time. Rebuilding trust isn't about a grand apology or a single truth that wipes the slate clean. It's about consistent, lived truth—in what you say and how you act.

If someone has lost trust in you, understand that they're allowed to take their time. You don't get to demand their forgiveness just because you've "decided to be honest now." Trust isn't built with words—it's built with action.

So be patient. Be consistent. Take accountability. And most importantly: be honest not just to fix things, but because it's the kind of person you actually want to be.

Remember: honesty isn't about being perfect. It's about being true—to your fears, your feelings, your flaws. To your friends, your family, and yes, even the barista who doesn't need your life story but appreciates a genuine smile. It means showing up as yourself, even when it's uncomfortable. Because every time you choose honesty, you're not just earning trust from others—you're building it within yourself.

When you compromise your integrity, you don't just risk your reputation. You chip away at your own peace. Small lies might feel like easy escapes, but they're like leaving banana peels on the floor. Eventually, you'll slip.

Growth comes from the harder choice. The one where you speak up, take responsibility, and stop performing. It's not glamorous. But it's powerful.

Think about the times you chose truth, even when it cost you. The relief. The alignment. The freedom that came from not carrying the lie anymore.

Skip the shortcuts. Say the uncomfortable thing (kindly). Show up for yourself with truth.

You're not too fragile for the truth. You're too powerful to keep hiding from it.

RULE #8:

Do the Thing

I almost didn't write this chapter. Not because I had nothing to say—but because *doing the thing* is hard. Especially when the thing is writing about *doing the thing.*

If procrastination were an Olympic sport, I wouldn't just have gold medals—I'd have endorsement deals and a signature shoe.

From the homework I swore I'd do during recess, to the unread emails that quietly aged into digital fossils, to the dentist appointment I've rescheduled three times because "next month feels better"—I've creatively mastered the art of avoidance.

And sure, it feels harmless at first. What's one more hour? One more day? But suddenly that "later" turns into never, and now you're three iced coffees deep at 1am questioning every life choice that led to this moment. Waiting doesn't just delay the work—it multiplies the dread. It turns a simple task into an existential crisis, and a mild inconvenience into full-blown chaos.

The cost? Wasted time. Missed opportunities. And a mountain of stress that future-you definitely did not ask for.

The funny thing about avoidance? It sneaks up on you so quietly you barely notice. It's not like you wake up and think, "Today, I'm going to avoid all my responsibilities and push the boundaries of chaos." No—it starts small. A text you'll reply to later. A task you'll do "when you're in the right mood." That closet you've been meaning to clean but have conveniently decided no longer exists.

Before you know it, your to-do list looks like it's auditioning for a horror movie—bloated, relentless, and definitely out for blood. Suddenly, you're lying awake at night wondering how things spiraled this far out of control.

The longer you wait, the bigger everything feels. Even simple tasks start to look like Everest. And all because you told yourself you'd do it "tomorrow."

And speaking of Everest, facing the mental resistance often feels like staring up at a towering mountain. The peak is barely visible, shrouded in clouds of doubt and dread. You stand at the base, wondering how on earth you'll ever reach the top.

No one summits a mountain in a single leap. The only way up is one step at a time. The climb looks impossible when you fixate on the finish line, but it gets manageable the moment you start moving.

That's the key to getting unstuck: start small, and let action build momentum.

The good news? Procrastination isn't a character trait—it's a habit. And like any habit, it can be broken.

The first step is figuring out why you're avoiding the thing. That's where self-awareness comes in. You've got to pause long enough to ask, "Okay… what's actually going on here?"

Maybe it's fear. Maybe it's overwhelm. Maybe your brain short-circuits the second you open your calendar. Whatever the reason, calling it out gives you a better shot at breaking the cycle.

Let's talk about fear. Most of the time, procrastination isn't laziness—it's discomfort avoidance. You're not running from the task itself; you're afraid of what it represents: the risk of failure, the pressure to be perfect, the vulnerability of actually trying.

And while procrastination feels like self-protection, all it really does is delay the discomfort and multiply the stress. Avoiding hard things doesn't make them disappear—it just gives them time to grow teeth.

The fix? Shrink the task until it feels manageable. Don't think "finish the thing," just think "start." Set a 10-minute timer and work until it goes off. That's it. No perfection, no pressure—just movement.

It's like dipping your toe into a freezing pool. You flinch. Everything in you says nope. But then you ease in a little more, and your body starts to adjust. The shock fades. Suddenly, it's bearable. Maybe even kind of refreshing. That first step—awkward and uncomfortable as it feels—is what makes the next one possible.

Even the tiniest win—a sentence written, a quick email sent, a sock finally picked up off the floor—can kickstart momentum. And that changes everything.

Now, let's talk about the consequences of delay. Delaying something might feel like relief, but it's fake peace. The task you're avoiding doesn't disappear—it just lingers, taking up mental space and creating low-grade stress that follows you like a shadow. And when the deadline finally hits? You're scrambling, panicking, and wondering why you didn't start sooner.

It's a cycle that feeds itself, leaving you exhausted and frustrated. And the worst part? That stress doesn't stay in its lane—it spills into everything else, making your whole life feel heavier than it needs to be.

I'll never forget the time I procrastinated writing a huge essay for English class. It had been on the syllabus for weeks, but I kept telling myself I'd knock it out later. Instead, I spent my afternoons scrolling social media and clinging to the lie that I "worked better under pressure."

Cut to the night it was due: I was hunched over my desk, the clock ticking closer to midnight, heart racing while I typed like a maniac—deleting, retyping, sweating, spiraling. I submitted it to Canvas at 11:58 PM. Technically on time. Barely.

And yeah, I actually got a good grade. But that's not the point. The stress I endured? Totally avoidable. There's a special kind of relief that comes with finishing something early—or even just on time—and that night, I realized how much I'd been missing out on by waiting until the last possible second.

That was just one paper. One mess of a night. But it taught me something important: avoidance doesn't just waste time—it chips away at your confidence. It gives you a false sense of peace that you will 1000% regret later.

And if that's what happens with one school assignment… what does it mean for the bigger stuff? The ideas we put off. The conversations we avoid. The dreams we keep on a shelf, waiting for a "someday" that never comes.

For years, I wanted to learn Swift coding and build iPhone apps. It was something I talked about constantly—planned for, dreamed about, imagined a thousand different ways. But every time I thought about starting, I'd tell myself I wasn't ready. *"I'll start when I have more time."* or *"I'm not good enough to be a real coder."*

Days turned into months. Months into years. I watched tutorials, read articles, told myself I was "getting closer"—but really, I was just circling the runway. I wasn't afraid of failing. I was afraid of starting.

One day, I looked up and realized I had spent more time thinking about learning to code than actually doing it. I had been stealing time from my own dreams—convincing myself that preparation was progress, when really, I was just avoiding the work.

The regret hit hard. Not just because I hadn't started—but because I believed I had more time than I did. And that belief cost me.

"That's tomorrow-me's problem" is the ultimate excuse. But tomorrow-you already has enough going on. Don't stack more on their plate.

It's a tempting mindset—it buys you comfort in the moment, but it dumps the consequences on someone who's already juggling too much. And that someone is still you. When you delay, you're handing your future self more stress, more pressure, and less breathing room. Why not make their life easier? Start the thing. Send the email. Fold the laundry. Think of it as a favor you're doing for yourself.

So how do you break the cycle? Lower the friction between you and the action. Make the first step automatic—whether that's keeping your gym bag in the car, pre-writing your to-do list the night before, or blocking focus time on your calendar.

If it's part of your system, you're not relying on willpower. You're just showing up—one simple, low-pressure step at a time.

And when you fall off track (because you will), meet yourself with compassion. Shame doesn't fix anything. It just keeps you stuck.

Acknowledge the delay, reset, and move forward. Progress isn't about being flawless—it's about refusing to quit.

Every moment is a reset button. Just don't use that as an excuse to keep hitting snooze on your life. (Yes, I see you. And yes, I'm judging… with love.)

Sometimes, the best way to combat procrastination is to embrace a simple mindset: *"Why not now?"* When you're tempted to put something off, ask yourself what's really stopping you. Most of the time, the reasons are flimsy at best—low energy, fear of imperfection, or just plain inertia. But when you challenge those excuses, you often realize the task isn't as big or scary as it felt. And once you've taken that first step, you'll wonder why you ever hesitated in the first place.

And once you're moving, celebrate that. Small victories matter. Every task you complete—no matter how minor—is momentum. Did you respond to all your emails? Grab your favorite snack. Finally cleaned out that drawer of doom? Take a second to bask in your own glory. Little rewards reinforce good habits, and they help shift your mindset from avoidance mode to achievement mode.

Think of it like giving a toddler candy for using the potty. Positive reinforcement works. And yes, potty procrastination is real. (Trust me, I still struggle with that one.) But the same principle applies to all of us. Sometimes we just need a little incentive to get moving—even if it's as simple as checking something off the list and basking in that sweet, momentary peace.

The trick is pairing those little wins with consistent action—so procrastination doesn't stand a chance.

Getting things done isn't about hustle. It's about balance. It's knowing when to push and when to pause. When to give yourself grace, and when to give yourself a little nudge. Doing the thing doesn't mean doing everything—it just means taking the next step, even when it's uncomfortable. Especially then.

Sure, procrastination feels like avoidance. But what you're really avoiding isn't the task—it's the discomfort wrapped around it. And it's not just about chasing big dreams—sometimes, it's about the moments we miss because we assume we'll always have more time.

Once, I had feelings for someone, but I kept putting off saying anything. I told myself I was waiting for the "perfect moment," that if I held out just a little longer, the right opportunity would show up. But time passed, and I kept stalling. *Maybe they didn't feel the same. Maybe I'd embarrass myself. Maybe it isn't meant to be.*

I convinced myself that waiting was safer—that holding back was smarter than risking rejection. And then one day, they moved on. Just like that, the door I'd been standing in front of for months quietly closed.

I remember sitting there afterward, realizing I hadn't been waiting—I'd been hiding. The regret wasn't just about what I lost. It was about knowing I let fear make the decision for me. I didn't just miss a moment. I missed the chance to even find out.

That kind of regret—the kind rooted in silence, in all the words you never said—is its own kind of weight.

Whether it's a dream you delay or a conversation you avoid, procrastination doesn't just steal time. It steals *possibility*. And the worst part? You don't always know what it takes from you until it's already gone.

But here's what you do get to control: the next step. The next decision. Facing things head-on isn't about checking off a to-do list—it's about building something stronger: resilience, confidence, and a life that actually feels like yours. Every time you act, even if it's small, you remind yourself you're capable of more than avoidance.

Ease in. Forgive yourself when you fall behind. And remember—action, even if it's awkward, unfinished, or uncomfortable, will always move you further than staying frozen.

Procrastination doesn't just steal your time—it steals your momentum. The only way to take that power back is to begin. Not because it's urgent. But because it matters. Because it's yours.

Freedom doesn't mean much if you never start building the life you want to be free in.

And the longer you wait? The heavier it gets.

Whatever's waiting for you—don't overthink it. Don't stall. Don't make it bigger than it is. Just do the thing.

Start now—before silence becomes your answer.

RULE #9:

Keep the Real Ones

I've had two friendships that shaped me in opposite ways. One cracked me open—taught me how to live louder, laugh harder, take up space. The other gave me room to fall apart. No expectations. No fixing. Just presence. One helped me find my voice. The other reminded me I didn't always have to use it.

That's the magic of friendship—you get to choose who gets close. And the best ones? They make you feel more you. Not less.

But let's be honest: we don't always choose with that kind of clarity. Sometimes we drift into friendships out of habit or proximity, never stopping to ask: Does this person actually see me? Support me? Accept me?

Because there's a difference between someone who laughs with you and someone who listens when you cry. Between someone who hypes you up and someone who holds you up.

Your friends shape your world more than you might realize. They influence your habits, your mindset, your mannerisms, and even your mood. Ever notice how spending an afternoon with someone who's perpetually negative leaves you feeling like you want complain too? On the flip side, hanging out with someone who radiates positivity can make the whole world seem a little brighter. It's a simple equation: good friends equal a better and happier you.

Finding real connection also means being intentional. Let's start with what really matters: quality over quantity. It might seem cool to have a hundred friends, but if you can't count on any of them to pick you up from the airport, what's the point? A few close, meaningful friendships trump a sea of superficial connections any day. These are the people who'll celebrate your wins, grieve your losses, and tell you when you've got spinach in your teeth. Treasure them.

This became clear to me when I was 14 and I met someone who completely changed my world. At the time, I was an awkward kid with only a handful of friends, but when I met her, everything shifted. We clicked instantly—becoming inseparable almost overnight. We went everywhere together, shared everything, and laughed until our stomachs hurt. People even assumed we were dating (spoiler: we weren't, and we quickly decided we were better off as friends). She was vibrant, unpredictable, and had the kind of contagious energy that could turn even the dullest moment into an adventure.

She made everything electric. A late-night Wendy's run for Frosties could turn into an impromptu therapy session or a deep dive into the meaning of life. Car rides became full-blown concerts—windows down, One Direction blasting, both of us belting lyrics like we were on tour. Plans didn't really exist with her. One minute we were grabbing snacks, the next we were two towns over, caught in some bizarre chain of spontaneous detours that somehow always made for the kind of story you had to start with, "Okay, you're not gonna believe this, but..."

That was her gift. She made the world feel like it was begging to be explored. And when I was with her, I said yes to everything. I felt funnier. Braver. Louder. Like my life had color again.

For years, she was my anchor. And then, one day, she wasn't. After high school, we stayed connected for a while, but at some point, she pulled away completely. No explanation. No slow fade. Just silence. I was devastated. I replayed every conversation, every moment, wondering what I had done wrong. Maybe I had leaned on her too much when I was going through a rough time? Maybe she didn't have the patience to deal with me anymore? Maybe life just got in the way? I'll never know for sure—and that's something I had to learn to live with.

It took me a long time to heal from that loss.

Losing a best friend like that felt less like a breakup and more like a funeral. No closure. No clean goodbye. Just silence where laughter used to live. I couldn't stop replaying things in my head—memories that once felt warm now felt like paper cuts. Grieving someone who was still alive but no longer part of my life is a strange kind of heartbreak. There's no apology. No reconciliation. Just the ache of not knowing why it ended—and the sharpness of realizing they chose not to explain.

And yet, with time, the ache softened. When I look back now, I don't feel the loss, I feel gratitude. She pushed me outside my comfort zone, made me more confident, and taught me how to embrace the moment. She shaped me in ways I didn't fully understand until long after she was gone.

She shifted something in me. Being around her made me braver—like maybe I didn't have to overthink everything to be worth being around. I started taking more chances, laughing at the wrong moments, saying yes before I had a plan. And yeah, some of that confidence came from her. But a lot of it was mine—I just needed someone to remind me it was already there.

Learning to move on from that loss changed how I approached relationships. I stopped seeing lost friendships as failures and started appreciating them for what they were: chapters in my story that helped shape who I am today. It doesn't make them any less valuable.

Of course, not all friendships are built to last forever, and that's okay. People grow, priorities shift, and sometimes, the healthiest thing you can do is let go. Recognizing red flags—like constant negativity, toxic behavior, or a lack of respect—is part of protecting your peace. If someone consistently makes you feel small, stressed, or unworthy, it's worth asking: "Is this friendship still serving me?" Walking away isn't easy, but sometimes, it's the most loving thing you can do—for both yourself and them.

And while we're here, let's talk about another kind of friendship breakdown: the one where you're doing all the work. When you're always the one texting first. Always making the plans. Always checking in while they keep disappearing. If that sounds familiar, it might be time to ask yourself some hard questions.

True friendship shouldn't feel like a solo mission. It's about balance—not showing up in identical ways, but showing up. When both people are invested, the connection becomes a loop of trust and support, not a slow leak that drains your energy and patience. The balance isn't in the math—it's in the mutual willingness to show up, again and again, even when life makes it inconvenient. Even when it's hard.

Letting go of toxic friendships is hard—but building the good ones takes guts, too. Real friendship is a quiet kind of bravery. It's saying, "I've got you," and actually meaning it.

Intention is a great start, but it's not the whole picture. Strong friendships take time, effort, and the kind of presence that can't be faked.

My favorite conversations usually happen late at night, outside, under the moonlight. There's something about the quiet air that makes it easier to be genuine. That's when my friends and I say the honest stuff—the stuff we'd never drop in a group chat. We listen without trying to fix, speak without fear of judgment, and show up with nothing to prove.

Those are the moments when friendships deepen—not just because of what's said, but because of the trust that lives in the silence between the words. Some of my strongest bonds were built during those small, sacred windows of honesty—when someone finally said, "I'm not okay right now," and we didn't look away.

For the longest time, I didn't talk about what was going on at home. I felt like I had to hold everything together—keep the peace, smooth over the drama, step in when things got out of control. Even though I was the youngest, I somehow became the referee. The fixer. The emotional buffer between people who should've been able to manage their own problems. I knew it wasn't supposed to be my responsibility... but I carried it anyway.

I never told anyone how heavy it all felt—until one night, it cracked. I was sitting in my car outside my best friend's house, and before I even knew what was happening, the words just spilled out. I told him everything: how I felt trapped, how I didn't know how to escape it, how exhausting it was to be the one always trying to hold everything together. I expected him to give me advice. Or tell me to let it go. But he didn't. He just sat there and listened. And for the first time in a long time, I didn't feel like I had to carry it alone.

That's the thing about true friendships—they don't always fix what's broken. But they remind you that you don't have to break with it. He gave me an escape, not by pretending my problems didn't exist, but by reminding me that life wasn't just what happened within my four walls. He made me laugh when I wanted to shut down. And he saw me when I felt invisible.

Not every friendship-defining moment is heavy. Sometimes, it's the simple, stupid, beautiful ones that remind you why these people matter.

Whether it's a spontaneous road trip, a late-night deep dive into absurd topics, or binge-watching a terrible Netflix series together, those are the moments that become the glue.

Shared laughter, especially, is a powerful bond. You know it's real when you're doubled over in hysterics over something so dumb you can't even explain why it's funny.

Friendship isn't always neat or tidy, but it's one of life's greatest privileges. Choosing friends with intention means surrounding yourself with people who inspire, challenge, and uplift you—and being open with them allows that bond to deepen in ways that bring out the best in you both.

Friendship is more than just who makes you laugh—it's who makes you feel authentic. Who reminds you you're not too much, or not enough. Who sees you fully… and stays.

So take a moment to reflect: who lights up your world? Who challenges you, supports you, and helps you grow?

Invest in them.

And who dims your shine? Who leaves you feeling small, unseen, or unsettled?

It might be time to let them go.

Because the people you surround yourself with don't just influence your life—they co-write it.

Just like my friend from high school helped me come out of my shell. Just like the one who gave me space to breathe when

I couldn't do it alone. Every friendship leaves a mark. Every connection adds another brushstroke to who you're becoming.

You don't have to fear the impermanence of it all. Some people are meant to walk beside you forever. Others are just passing through.

But what matters isn't how long someone stays—it's how they showed up while they were there. The way they held space. The way they reminded you who you were when you forgot.

So choose wisely. And choose with an open heart.

Because friendship isn't about perfection. It's about presence. The ones who stay when things get awkward, hard, or heavy. The ones who don't flinch when you're not okay.

It's about laughing until you cry… and crying until you laugh again.

And yeah—maybe keeping a friend or two on standby for your next IKEA adventure. Because in the end, it's not about having perfect directions.

It's about who's in the car with you—turning up the music, passing the snacks, and sticking around even when nothing makes sense.

RULE #10:

Balance Aspiration with Satisfaction

I've spent years running after the next milestone—thinking the next version of success would finally make me feel like I'd made it. But no matter how much I crossed off the list, that feeling never showed up. At least, not the way I expected.

One day it hit me: I wasn't aiming for a goal—I was chasing a feeling. Validation. Security. That elusive breath of "Ah, now I'm enough." But every time I got close, the target moved. The promotion came with new pressure. The trip ended. The applause faded. And I was right back where I started: hungry for more.

That's when I started paying attention—not to what I wanted next, but to what was already in front of me.

There's a difference between ambition and addiction. One pulls you forward. The other keeps you sprinting in circles, hoping the next big thing will finally fill the gap.

This rule isn't about giving up your goals. It's about building a life where joy doesn't wait at the finish line.

The issue isn't wanting more—it's tethering your peace to the next big milestone. That job. That trip. That perfect version of your life that you keep imagining. It'll never be enough if you don't pause to feel proud of what you've already done.

Achievement fades fast if you don't let it land. Satisfaction is what anchors you. It's not the end of progress—it's what makes progress feel like it matters.

A few years back, I planned a week-long trip to San Diego and Los Angeles with two of my friends. We had a jam-packed itinerary: the San Diego Zoo, Sea World, a show at the Pantages Theatre, even a concert at the Hollywood Bowl. We were constantly on the move, checking things off the list, trying to squeeze every drop out of the experience. And while it was an incredible trip, those aren't the moments I think about most.

My favorite day? The one where we slowed down. We spent an afternoon at Coronado Beach, just off the coast of San Diego. The sun was warm, the breeze was cool, and the only sound was the steady rhythm of the waves. We had nowhere to be, nothing to prove, and nothing on the schedule. We just sat. Talked. Reflected on the trip, on life back home, on how good it felt to be fully in that moment.

That single afternoon, more than any of the big events, is what I remember most. Because for once, we weren't even thinking about the next thing—we were just there. And that presence? That was the real magic.

It didn't mean I had no goals or ambition. It just reminded me that growth doesn't always look like motion. That sometimes, the best thing you can do is pause and feel it.

And that's the key: balance. Aspiration isn't the enemy. It's what keeps life interesting. It pushes us to grow, to test our limits, to turn vision into reality.

But unchecked ambition? That's where things get tricky. It can leave you burned out, restless, and constantly convinced you're not doing enough—no matter how much you're actually doing.

The key is knowing when to push forward and when to pause. Think of ambition as the engine that moves you—and satisfaction as the brake that lets you slow down and actually enjoy the ride.

You need both if you want to stay on the road without crashing.

I learned this lesson (again) after upgrading my iPhone for the seventh year in a row. I'll admit it: I have a problem. Each time, I convinced myself that the new model was essential—because of some barely upgraded camera, a gimmicky new button, or a slightly shinier color.

And yeah, the first week was great. I played with all the new stuff. Took unnecessary portrait photos of plants. Bragged about the Action Button. But pretty soon, it all started to feel exactly like last year's phone—and the excitement faded. Fast.

What stuck with me wasn't the phone. It was the headache of setting everything up again. It was the realization that I'd swapped out stability for a buzz that barely lasted a week.

And what actually brought me joy? Not the tech. Not the specs. It was laughing with my friends about how ridiculous my annual upgrade habit had become. It was realizing they didn't care what phone I had—they just liked me. As-is.

That moment was humbling. And it reminded me: the best stuff in life doesn't come in a box. It shows up in connection, in presence, in learning how to appreciate what's already right in front of you.

The people who matter most? They don't care how polished you look or how impressive your feed is. They care about *you*. About how you make them feel. That's where real satisfaction lives.

When you prioritize connection over status, you don't just find more joy—you remember that satisfaction isn't about having more. It's about being known. And when you stop measuring your worth by what you own or how "relevant" you are, you make space for relationships that are actually real.

Social media only makes this harder. It's easy to tie your value to likes, shares, and followers—easy to believe that the numbers say something about who you are.

But that kind of validation? It's a moving target. You hit one milestone, and suddenly it's on to the next. The goalposts never stop shifting.

And none of it—*none of it*—says anything about your character, your depth, or your worth. The people who matter are the ones who see beyond the feed. The ones who stick around whether your posts pop off or flop completely.

Forget the follower count. Focus on the people who text you back, laugh at your dumb jokes, and check in when you go quiet. Those are the ones that count.

Satisfaction isn't settling. It's knowing when to stop reaching long enough to appreciate what's already in your hands. It's the part where you look around and realize: this is actually pretty good.

Gratitude helps with that—but not the performative kind. The real kind. The kind that sneaks up on you when the sun hits just right or someone makes you laugh so hard you forget why you were stressed in the first place.

Start small: the comfort of a hoodie that fits just right, the way your friend says your name, the last line of a really good book. Ordinary things. Easy to miss. But they add up.

Try keeping a running list in your Notes app. Nothing fancy. Just the little moments that made you smile, surprised you, or reminded you that maybe—just maybe—you're doing alright. The more specific, the better.

Do it long enough, and something shifts. You stop scanning for what's missing. You start noticing what's enough.

Not every day has to change your life. Sometimes the win is just showing up. Doing the thing you said you would. Sending the email. Cleaning the kitchen. Having one real conversation. Some days just need to feel real. That's enough.

Joy isn't waiting for you somewhere down the line. It's already here—if you're willing to look for it. Gratitude doesn't cancel ambition. It grounds it. It reminds you to move forward with clarity instead of sprinting after a goal that keeps moving the second you get close.

Aspiration still matters. It's what keeps us moving, dreaming, evolving.

Let your goals add to your life—not consume it. Set bold intentions, but break them into steps you can actually take. Celebrate milestones instead of waiting until the finish line to feel proud.

That mindset turns ambition into fuel—not fire. And remember: progress matters more than perfection.

When you tip too far in either direction, things fall apart.

Focus only on satisfaction, and you risk getting stuck. Focus only on ambition, and you'll burn out pursuing things that never feel like enough.

The sweet spot is in the middle. That rhythm—between reaching and resting—is what creates a life that's sustainable. Driven, but not depleted. Content, but not asleep.

And when you feel yourself slipping into "what's next?" mode, hit pause and ask:

Why do I want this?

Is this mine—or am I doing it because I think I'm supposed to?

A lot of the time, the thing we're reaching for isn't even ours. It's a story we absorbed. A standard we inherited. But when you redirect that energy—toward moments that actually fill you up, like time with your people, work that fuels you, or a quiet joy you don't have to post about—that's where real satisfaction lives.

So stop measuring your life against someone else's highlight reel. Pay attention to your lane. Your pace. Your progress.

And while you're at it? Acknowledge what's already working. (Seriously. You're probably doing better than you think.)

Too often, we move the goalposts without even noticing. You land the job—and five minutes later, you're stressed about the next promotion. You finish the big project—then immediately spiral about what's next.

Pause. Breathe it in. Let yourself feel the win.

Book the dinner. Take the guilt-free day off. Satisfaction isn't laziness—it's the exhale you earned for showing up and doing the work.

In the end, balancing aspiration with satisfaction is about redefining success. It's not about having it all. It's about having enough—and knowing it. It's about wanting more without needing to rush. Growing without always grasping. Letting ambition stretch you without letting it swallow you.

Life's too short to miss it because you're busy trying to outrun it.

So ask yourself: What truly brings you joy? What do you already have that you're grateful for? And what dreams are worth pursuing—not because they'll make you more valuable, but because they'll make your life richer? That's the balance: purpose *and* peace.

Aspire to be better, but don't forget to enjoy the life you're already living.

When ambition wears you out, that's your cue. Pause. Breathe. Sit in the stillness—not because your work is done, but because you've earned a breath to remember *why* it matters. Sometimes, rest is the reward. Let yourself receive it.

Satisfaction isn't the end of ambition. It's the soil your next dream grows from. It's the breath between breakthroughs—the part that makes progress feel like *presence*, not pressure.

Because if you're always reaching for what's next, you'll never realize you're already standing in the middle of something you once dreamed about.

Stop for a second. Look around—and *live* it.

PART 3:
Live Out Loud

Okay, you've done the work. You've faced the mirror, called yourself out, maybe even cried in a Target parking lot (no judgment—I've been there). You've stripped back the layers, challenged the stories, survived the emotional rollercoaster of self-awareness.

Now comes the fun part: actually being that person out loud.

This section is where things get bold. A little rebellious. Maybe even a little unhinged—in the best way. It's about choosing yourself loudly, living like you mean it, and letting the world adjust to who you actually are.

No more shrinking to fit. No more playing it cool to avoid being "too much." These next few rules are here to remind you: you're allowed to be seen. To take up space. To live a life that feels like yours, not just one that photographs well.

This isn't about performing confidence—it's about owning your wholeness. Even the messy parts. Especially the messy parts.

So turn up the volume.

It's time to live out loud.

RULE #11:

Never Forget Who You Are

I feel like I wasted my 20s. They're almost over, and I keep looking back wondering where all that time went. I blinked and a decade disappeared. And still—so many dreams unrealized. Instead, my days were passed analyzing my personality, always trying to be everything at once—unique but not weird, original but still relatable, successful but not elitist.

I spent years putting off risks, second-guessing creative ideas, obsessing over image instead of impact. I obsessed over validation in work, in friendships, in places that always left me emptier than before.

Looking back to when I was a teenager, I imagined myself as a big-shot creative at a tech company, always on the edge of something new. When I should've been listening to the teacher, I was daydreaming about wealth, travel, stability—the kind of life where I could provide for a beautiful family and build something meaningful for myself and others.

But somewhere along the way, I got lost. Not all at once—just a little at a time. I adapted. I toned things down. Traded hot takes for half-smiles. Said "totally!" when I meant "not really." I laughed at jokes I didn't think were funny. Rewrote texts until they sounded like everyone else's. Swapped outfits that made me feel alive for ones that made me invisible. Hid the weird socks. Downplayed the fact that The Legend of Zelda practically raised me. Kept quiet about the music that made me cry in parking lots. Closed my Notes app like my ideas were secrets. Said I was being easygoing. But really, I was dialing myself down until there was barely anything left.

And I told myself I was still me. Just… easier to like.

The more I diluted myself, the less I recognized the person in the mirror. I wasn't evolving—I was shape-shifting for approval. I let other people's comfort become my compass.

Somewhere along the way, I stopped checking in with my own intuition. Stopped asking what I actually wanted. Stopped trusting what felt like mine. And somewhere in that slow drift toward "likable," I stopped feeling real.

Here's what no one tells you: when you spend all your energy trying to blend in, you lose the thread. You forget your own goals, your own instincts. And before you know it, you're a zombie—mindlessly scrolling through life, wondering when you even became this person.

Time is weird. One second you're dreaming about the future, and the next you're staring at the clock wondering where the last decade went. And the thing about time? It doesn't hand out do-overs. The real tragedy isn't just in the years lost—it's in realizing how many of them you spent living for someone else.

Losing yourself isn't some big dramatic break. It's quieter. A skipped joke here, a swallowed opinion there. A quiet shelving of something you love because it's "not realistic." It adds up before you even notice.

Then one day, you look in the mirror and realize you've been editing yourself for so long you don't even remember the unfiltered version. Who even is this person? Did I create them... or was I algorithmically generated by the expectations of society and my parents?

Society is loud. Always telling you what success looks like, what kind of life you should want, who you should be.

Fit in. Be likable. Don't be too different—but don't be boring either. Be successful, but stay humble. Speak your mind—unless it makes people uncomfortable. Blend in. Stand out. Be bold. Be safe. No wonder we're exhausted.

And don't forget to drink enough water, maintain a 10-step skincare routine, read five books a month, and somehow still get 8 hours of sleep.

No pressure.

The rules are impossible. Constantly shifting, totally contradictory—and still, we try to follow them, hoping that if we do everything just right, we'll finally feel like we belong.

But belonging was never meant to be earned. It's not about fitting a mold. It's about staying whole. The right people won't ask you to tone yourself down to be accepted—they'll make space for you as you are.

The true risk isn't the awkward interactions or uncomfortable silences. It's that you'll go silent inside yourself.

But how do you know when it's happening? Maybe you find yourself agreeing to avoid conflict—even when your gut says otherwise. You smile and nod, not because you agree, but because it's easier. At first, it feels like no big deal. But over time, those small edits chip away at your voice until it doesn't sound like you anymore.

Or maybe you've started downplaying your wins, dimming your personality to keep others comfortable. You call it humility, but underneath, it's fear—fear of standing out, fear of being misunderstood, fear of making other people squirm. And the more you pull back, the more disconnected you feel—even from yourself.

I used to avoid telling people I was working on a book. I'd say I was "just experimenting with ideas" or "dabbling in some writing"—like if I played it casual enough, it wouldn't sting if they didn't take it seriously. Like ambition was something I had to downplay to keep the room comfortable.

But it wasn't humility—it was fear. Fear of sounding delusional. Fear of failing in public. Fear of someone raising an eyebrow and going, "Oh. Cute."

It took me way too long to realize: downplaying your dreams doesn't protect them. It just dims them before they even begin.

I still remember the first time I said it out loud—"I'm writing a book." No qualifiers. No disclaimers. Just the truth. And the second I said it, something clicked. It finally felt true. Like I'd finally given myself permission to believe it.

And honestly? I wish I'd said it sooner. Turns out, once you stop editing your dreams, you start noticing how much else you've been watering down too. There's hesitation before you speak—that flicker of doubt. You soften your words, tweak your tone, second-guess your opinions—not because they're wrong, but because you're afraid of being "too much."

We're wired to adapt. That's not weakness—it's survival. Your personality shifts a little with your parents, your coworkers, your old high school friends. Adapting is necessary—but so is staying anchored.

When you lose that anchor, you don't just adapt—you drift. You start performing instead of participating. Curating instead of connecting. You wear what feels safe, say what won't get side-eyed, and dodge anything that might make you look weird or complicated. And somewhere in that performance, the things that used to light you up—your obscure music playlists, your fanfic drafts, your homemade cosplay outfits with far too much commitment—they start to fade. You tell yourself you've outgrown them. But really? You just stopped making room.

Think of all the people you turned away from who would've loved the real you, if you'd just had the guts to show up as them.

If any of this feels familiar, it's not too late. It's just your cue to pause. To check in. To start making your way back.

Forgetting who you are isn't permanent. You can always find your way back—it just takes intention.

The first step? Remember who you were before the world told you who to be.

I think about that version of me—the barefoot kid riding his bike through the Arizona heat, singing at full volume with zero shame, writing fanfiction like it was my full-time job. The one hosting Mario Kart marathons and choreographing imaginary movie trailers with his friends. I built entire worlds out of LEGOs and cardboard boxes, read until my eyes ached, and swam shirtless without thinking twice about what I looked like. I was loud. I was weird. I was unstoppable. And my friends? They didn't just tolerate that version of me—they looked up to him. Because I wasn't trying to be anyone else. I was already enough.

That version of me—the one who created without fear, who dreamed without limits—is still in there. You don't need permission to be him again. You just have to stop pretending he was a phase.

Then, start noticing what lights you up now.

Forget what sounds impressive. Pay attention to what actually pulls you in. What YouTube tabs are you always reopening? What stories do you bring up unprompted? What's the thing you keep saying you'll "get back into someday" even though it's been five years?

For me, it was writing scenes in the Notes app that no one asked for, geeking out over app design and Swift tutorials, and rearranging playlists like they were mixtapes for an imaginary movie. That wasn't procrastination—it was memory. It was my curiosity quietly trying to lead me home.

You don't need to explain your joy. You just need to follow it.

Next, surround yourself with the right people.

You know the ones. The friends who send you memes at 2am that are somehow both hilarious and deeply validating. The ones who've seen you cry on the bathroom floor and still think you're a force. The people who don't shrink when you show your full intensity—they match it.

I think about the friends who stayed up with me until 4am talking about big dreams and dumb fears. The ones who reminded me I was allowed to say yes—even when I had no idea what came next. The ones who showed up with ice cream even when I had pushed them away. That kind of safety net? That kind of presence? That's the real flex.

If they need you to be different to feel comfortable, they're not your people. Keep walking.

And finally, stop apologizing for being too much.

I used to read a room like a script—calculating every word, every joke, every outfit. God forbid I say the wrong thing or come across "extra." But eventually I realized: in trying to be palatable, I'd made myself unrecognizable.

You're not here to be more digestible (we have TUMS for that). You're here to be honest.

Allow yourself to be the person who sends voice memos that are way too long. Who brings up existential questions in the middle of Taco Bell. Who dresses up fancy for no reason. Who laughs too loud, feels too deeply, and dares to be enthusiastic in a world that worships cool indifference.

Be the kind of *too much* that feels like home. Because the people who matter? They won't ask you to alter yourself to be something safer. They'll meet you where you are.

And they'll be better for it.

Honestly—why play it small for people who wouldn't recognize your brilliance anyway?

Reclaiming yourself isn't about reinventing everything overnight. It's about realizing that external validation is a game you were never meant to win. You reach one version of "acceptable," and suddenly the standard shifts again.

It's exhausting—constantly recalibrating who you are just to stay likable. Living for approval is like trying to win an argument in a group chat—emotionally draining, endlessly circular, and never actually satisfying.

What's the alternative? Act like you're on your own side. Not in a cocky way—in a quietly confident, *I've got me* kind of way.

If you wouldn't put up with a friend who constantly criticized you, dismissed your feelings, or forced you to be someone you're not, then why do it to yourself?

You're the one teaching people how to treat you—even when it's just you. The more you respect, understand, and accept who you are, the less you'll rely on the approval of people who don't even know the real you.

A good way to check in with yourself is to ask: Who am I when no one else is watching? What do I actually enjoy, outside of what's trendy? What opinions do I hold, even if they aren't the popular ones? What parts of myself have I been neglecting just to keep the peace?

If those questions feel uncomfortable, that's okay. Discomfort is often the first sign that you're getting closer to something real.

Here's a challenge: Take ten minutes today to sit with yourself—really sit. No distractions. No pretending.

Write down the things that make you *you*. Not the perfect, Insta-curated personality. Not the image you've been told is more acceptable. But the parts that feel truest—the ones that make you laugh when no one's watching, or cry when something hits a little too close.

The next time you're tempted to edit yourself to make others comfortable, revisit that list.

Let it remind you of one simple truth: You don't have to be less to be loved. You just have to be honest.

Being yourself isn't always easy. Sometimes, it means losing people who only liked the toned-down you. It might mean standing alone for a while, or feeling out of place when everyone else seems to be moving in sync. But the alternative, losing yourself completely, is far worse.

Speak your mind. Do the things that feel true to you, even if no one else gets it. Because the image of you they accept won't matter if it's not the one you can live with.

Never forget who you are.

The world will ask you to make sense. You weren't born to be simple.

You're not here to blend in. You're here to be real. Loud. Unedited. Fully alive.

And if you've lost yourself along the way, don't panic. You're not gone—you're just buried under expectations that were never yours to carry.

Start dismantling them, one unapologetic decision at a time.

Reclaim the kid the world tried to bury—the one who dreamed without limits, created without fear, and never asked if it was too much.

Let them lead like they never stopped.

Because deep down, they never did.

RULE #12:

Master the Unapology

A lot of us throw out "sorry" like we're handing out free samples at Costco. One time, I sneezed in an empty elevator and said, "Sorry." To the silence. To the air. To the judgmental ghosts of elevator etiquette past. And the worst part? I instantly felt embarrassed, like the elevator itself was judging me.

And it's not just elevators. The other day, I crossed the street at the crosswalk (like, legally) and when a car slowed down for me, I panicked and mouth-mumbled "Sorry" at the driver. FOR WHAT?! For walking where I was supposed to?

That's when I realized I had an unnecessary sorry problem. It had become a reflex. A filler. Something I tossed into conversations like an overused emoji. But apologizing isn't meant to be instinctive—it's meant to acknowledge when you've actually done something wrong. When "sorry" becomes the default, it stops being about empathy, and starts being about insecurity.

How many times had I said "sorry" just to make myself easier to tolerate? How often had I handed over space that was mine—just to avoid making waves?

Constantly apologizing for things that don't require an apology doesn't make you polite. It makes you seem like you're apologizing for existing. And you're not (or, well, you shouldn't be).

I decided right then: it was time to break up with unnecessary apologies—for good.

Real apologies matter. But that's not what this is about.

This is about the other kind—the ones we hand out for existing. For asking questions. For having needs. For showing emotion. For walking in the direction someone else wanted to walk.

It's time to cut that out.

I am the youngest in my family by several years, which meant I learned early on how to play the role of referee.

Not because anyone asked me to, but because I hated conflict. Nothing made me more anxious than hearing voices rise, feeling the tension in the air, knowing that an argument was bubbling just under the surface.

I was afraid of confrontation—actually, no, I was afraid of the outcome scenarios I made up in my head. I imagined fights escalating, people storming off, doors slamming, silence that lasted forever.

So I did what I could to keep things from ever getting that far. I became a fixer. A peacekeeper. And my number one tool? Apologizing. Even when I hadn't done anything wrong, saying "sorry" was the quickest way to shut it all down.

If I could smooth things over fast enough, maybe I wouldn't have to sit through the discomfort. It didn't matter if I was at fault—what mattered was keeping the peace. And it worked… for a while.

But the problem with always playing peacekeeper? You start absorbing blame that was never yours. You train yourself to take responsibility for other people's tension. And one day, without realizing it, you're apologizing for things that don't even make sense: "Sorry for asking a question." "Sorry I didn't text back fast enough." "Sorry for being in the way." "Sorry for needing anything at all."

Until one day, you catch yourself saying sorry to a stranger for existing too close to them in line at a coffee shop… and you think: *Wait. Why am I like this?*

We've all been there. But every needless sorry chips away at our confidence. It doesn't read as polite—it reads like you're bracing for a consequence that was never coming.

That stops now.

Apologizing is powerful—when it's warranted. But like any power, it loses its meaning when overused. Living unapologetically doesn't mean being inconsiderate or refusing to own your mistakes. It means recognizing that not every moment calls for an apology, and that confidence isn't about being loud—it's about knowing when to stand firm and when to make things right.

Over-apologizing isn't just a quirky habit—it's a survival strategy. One often born from insecurity, social conditioning, and a deep-seated desire to avoid conflict.

From a young age, many of us are taught that politeness means minimizing our presence. That keeping the peace means taking the blame. That being liked means never making anyone uncomfortable.

Over time, that conditioning hardens into a reflex. We say sorry when handing someone a pen they dropped. We apologize for squeezing past someone in a crowd, as if existing in public space is somehow offensive.

And the more we do it, the more natural it starts to feel—like guilt is the price of admission for taking up space.

What it actually does is train people to expect less from us. It teaches them to overlook our needs, doubt our confidence, and treat our voice like background noise.

And when every little thing gets a "sorry," the important ones lose their power.

Let's get something straight: true apologies are important. If you've actually hurt someone, messed up, or caused unnecessary inconvenience, then yes, own it. A genuine apology is about accountability, not just easing discomfort. But let's break the cycle of saying sorry for things that don't need fixing.

Instead of defaulting to an apology, try shifting your language:

Instead of: "Sorry I'm late."

Try: "Thanks for waiting for me."

Instead of: "Sorry, can I squeeze past you?"

Try: "Excuse me."

Instead of: "Sorry to bother you, but…"

Try: "Do you have a minute?"

This small shift makes a huge difference in how you come across. You're still polite, but now you're speaking with confidence instead of unnecessary guilt.

Apologies don't always come in words. They show up in how we hesitate, over-explain, or ask for approval that was never required.

These quiet, constant actions send a message: that we think we're a disruption. That our presence needs to be excused.

But that's not true. It never was.

If you've ever stepped into a room and instinctively minimized your presence, you know the weight of these silent apologies. But you don't need to justify your existence. You belong—fully, unapologetically, without permission.

Your past self would be in awe that you made it here. That alone is proof you belong.

Your body speaks even when you don't. Fidgeting, hesitating, or fading into the background can all feel like you're quietly saying:

"I'm sorry for being here."

But you don't need to soften yourself to deserve space. Stand tall. Speak with certainty. Own your presence. You are not an intrusion; you are meant to exist.

Let's make this crystal clear:

You do NOT need to apologize for having an opinion.

You do NOT need to apologize for setting boundaries.

You do NOT need to apologize for prioritizing your needs.

You do NOT need to apologize for showing up fully.

You do NOT need to apologize for being here.

And you definitely do NOT need to apologize for rewriting the rules.

Over-apologizing often stems from a need for external validation—a quiet attempt to earn acceptance, to preempt disapproval, to keep the peace.

But constantly saying "sorry" for existing won't earn you more respect. It reinforces the idea that you believe you're a burden.

True confidence is when you stop rehearsing your entrance and just walk in like it's your house.

There's a difference between humility and self-doubt. Humility lets you own your mistakes. Self-doubt convinces you to take blame for things that aren't yours.

Being unapologetic isn't selfish or rude. It's clarity. It's self-respect. It's knowing when to take responsibility—and when to stand your ground.

Never apologize for being yourself. The world will tell you to fit in, to smooth out your edges, to be more manageable.

Don't fall for it.

Speak your mind. Wear the outfit. Post the selfie. Take the last slice of pizza. Walk in the room like it was waiting for you. Because it was.

And if that makes someone uncomfortable?

That's their problem. Not yours.

I might still be the youngest, but I'm not the mascot, the buffer, or the emotional translator anymore. I'm done saying "sorry" for things that don't need fixing.

This is me—volume up, shoulders back, not flinching.

This doesn't just apply to me though. You've got your own comeback to make.

You're already bringing the inner kid back into the light. But the fear that buried them in the first place?

That part stays buried.

RULE #13:

Be the Hero of Your Own Story

Every great story needs a hero. And guess what? This one's yours. Your life isn't some background scene in someone else's adventure. You're not the NPC (Non-Player Character) standing in the corner, repeating the same tired dialogue while other people move the story forward. No—you're Player One. The one who takes risks, makes bold choices, and grows through every twist and turn.

I never thought of myself as a leader. Not in the traditional sense. But when I was a kid, I was that friend—the one organizing the games, assigning characters, mapping out missions like we were on some epic adventure. My ideas were usually a little over-the-top, but that was the fun of it. My friends didn't just follow along—they trusted me to take the lead.

Somewhere along the way, that kid started to fade. I got quieter. More agreeable. Less sure of my own ideas. I started waiting—waiting for someone to tell me what came next, to co-sign my choices, to hand me permission to move. I wasn't taking the lead anymore. I was hoping someone else would.

And no one noticed. Because I still showed up. Still smiled. But I wasn't leading—I was waiting.

That's what this rule is about. Not becoming the loudest person in the room or the face of the group project. It's about taking ownership of your own story. It's about noticing when you've stepped out of the driver's seat—and deciding to climb back in.

Before you grab your metaphorical sword and charge into battle, let's address the elephant in the room: Are you living like the lead of your story, or have you slipped into the role of passive observer? It's easier than you think to fall into NPC energy.

Everyone has potential—for societal impact, for joy, for becoming someone they're proud of. But potential means nothing if it never gets activated. You don't become the hero by waiting to feel ready. You become the hero by choosing to move even when you're terrified.

And if you don't? Life keeps moving without you. That's the part no one tells you. There's no "pause" button on becoming who you're meant to be. There's no crew of developers coming to fix your code. If you don't claim the lead, something else will—fear, perfectionism, expectations. And you'll still be in the story… just not the one you were meant to live.

Maybe you're coasting through the same routines, waiting for a "sign" to tell you what to do next. Maybe you've been following someone else's map, ignoring your own instincts.

This rule is about agency, yes. But deeper than that, it's about not ghosting your own life. Because if you don't step in, you'll still exist—just without momentum, without magic, and without meaning.

The good news? You don't need a rewrite—you just need to start pressing buttons. You've had the controller the whole time.

Here's the difference: main characters make decisions, face challenges, and adapt as life unfolds. NPCs, on the other hand, exist in the periphery. They're reactive, not proactive. They're the ones who say, "Sorry, I can't help you with that," while standing next to a literal treasure chest.

Don't be the NPC.

Think of a time when you found yourself waiting; waiting for someone to invite you, for an opportunity to fall into your lap, or for the "right moment" to take a leap. That's background-character behavior. The ones who take charge don't sit around. They create. They take risks, even when the outcome isn't guaranteed. Because that's what makes the story worth telling.

A few months ago, one of my favorite bands announced a tour. Tickets went on sale, and I was ready—laptop open, credit card in hand. I had been waiting for this for years.

But just before I clicked "Buy," I hesitated.

What if none of my friends wanted to go? What if I ended up there alone?

It felt weird to plan something just for myself, so I waited. I texted a few people, trying to find someone who was down.

By the time I got a response, it was too late. Sold out. Gone in minutes. And the resale tickets? Five to ten times the original price.

I sat there staring at the "Sold Out" banner, not just frustrated, but disappointed in myself. Because I knew this wasn't the first time I had done this.

I had spent so much of my life waiting. Waiting for people to validate my choices. Waiting for the "perfect moment" to do something. Waiting for someone else to make a decision for me so I wouldn't have to take the risk alone.

And every time I waited, I lost.

That's when it hit me: people who take ownership don't wait. They act. Even if it means showing up alone.

For years, I told myself that writing wasn't "practical." That it was just a side hobby, something I could do for fun—but not something people would actually care about.

Deep down, I loved it. But every time I thought about pursuing it seriously, this little voice in my head would shut it down:

You're not good enough. No one wants to read what you have to say. Why even try?

So, I didn't. I put it aside, convinced that if I just ignored the urge to write, it would stop nagging at me.

It didn't.

It took me years to realize that fear wasn't stopping me—permission was. And I was the one refusing to give it.

I was the one who handed over the pen and let fear write my story for me. But the plot twist? I took it back. And the second I decided to take it back—to believe in what I had to say—everything changed.

Choosing to finally write wasn't just about putting words on a page. It was about stepping into my own story, unapologetically. It was about realizing that I don't need permission to live like my voice mattered.

That's the power of claiming your role: when you stop waiting for someone to validate you, you start becoming the person you were always meant to be.

You already threw out society's rulebook—this is just your next move.

If you don't start owning the story, it'll keep defaulting to the generic version. And sure, you can survive like that. Pay your bills, post your updates, smile at the right angles. But you'll be haunted by this low-level ache that says, "There's supposed to be more than this." Because there is. But you only get there when you stop outsourcing your agency and start actually doing something with it.

Here's the truth: taking the lead isn't always glamorous. Sometimes it means making hard calls or facing awkward moments head-on. Other times, it's about realizing that life's best opportunities aren't labeled as "quests." They're hidden in plain sight, waiting for you to take the risk. The difference often comes down to who's willing to say, "*Why not?*" and dive into the unknown.

Being the hero doesn't mean life is easy. It's the challenges that make the journey worth remembering.

Imagine playing a video game with no enemies, no puzzles, no stakes. Boring, right? The same goes for life. Conflict is where growth happens. It's what shapes your character—on-screen and off.

Got rejected from a dream job? That's not the end. That's the inciting incident that pushes the story forward. Made a huge mistake? Welcome to the montage where you learn, adapt, and come back stronger.

Heroes aren't defined by their setbacks. They're defined by how they respond.

People who drive their own stories make choices. Everyone else waits for instructions. One of the most empowering things you can do is own your decisions, big or small. Sure, some of them will feel boss-level difficult, but every time you choose, you shape the narrative.

Start with one decision that's fully yours. Decide what you want your morning to look like—not what you think it *should* look like. Pick a hobby that actually lights you up—not one that's trending on TikTok this week. Say no to what drains you, even if it's uncomfortable.

Every choice you make reinforces the truth: this is your story. This isn't a cutscene. You're in it. You're moving the story forward.

No more waiting for someone else to press X to continue.

The small choices are where it starts—but at some point, you're going to hit a bigger moment. A fork in the road. And that's where real agency shows up. When everything in you says *wait*, but something deeper says *go anyway.*

That might mean starting a new career path, moving to a new city, or ending a toxic relationship. Whatever it is, remember: heroes take action. They don't wait for perfect conditions—because they know those conditions rarely exist.

The story's already happening, whether you're steering or not. Every time you say "maybe later," the next chapter starts writing itself anyway—just with way less input from you. And that's the thing no one warns you about: indecision is still a decision. Delay long enough, and you don't just miss out on the risk—you miss the part where you get to grow because of it.

That said, even the boldest decisions are easier to face when you know someone's in your corner. Taking the lead doesn't mean doing it solo. Even the most legendary heroes don't go it alone. Think about Frodo without Sam, or Mario without Luigi. Every main character has a squad. Your people matter.

They lift you up, challenge you, and remind you who you are when you're stuck in a metaphorical dungeon.

But here's the catch: you have to choose your allies wisely. Surround yourself with people who share your values, who celebrate your wins, and who aren't afraid to call you out when you're veering off track. Just like you wouldn't add an NPC with bad stats to your party, don't keep people around who burn you out or hold you back.

Your hero squad isn't just about support; it's about inspiration. When you surround yourself with people who strive for greatness in their own lives, it pushes you to level up, too. If your current circle feels more like a group of NPCs stuck in a loop, it might be time to recruit some new allies.

Comparison will try to derail you. Especially now, when everyone's life looks curated for applause and aesthetic. But your story isn't theirs. It doesn't have to follow the same plot points or hit the same milestones.

Success isn't about copying someone else's adventure. It's about owning your path—and all the weird, beautiful detours that come with it.

Progress isn't linear, and sometimes the side quests hold the most magic.

Maybe it's a new skill, a surprising friendship, or a moment of clarity about what you truly want. Don't rush through them just to get to the "main quest."

That's where the good stuff lives—the unexpected turns, the parts you didn't plan for but needed anyway.

Being the hero of your own story is about living intentionally. Recognizing that your choices, challenges, and triumphs add up to a life that's uniquely yours. It's about stepping out of the background and taking center stage—not because you're perfect, but because you're willing to show up. And that effort? That's what makes you a hero.

Instead of waiting for the perfect moment, make a move.

Pick one part of your life where you've been sitting on the sidelines—something you've been avoiding, downplaying, or waiting for someone else to initiate.

Do one small thing about it today, because nothing changes until you do.

You don't need a cape or a cue. You just need to stop waiting for permission.

The stakes are simple: if you don't live like the hero, no one else is going to do it for you. And you'll never know what your story could've been—only what it almost was.

The kid who once planned entire adventures from scratch? They're the one holding the map now. Let them show you the way.

No more waiting. No more NPC energy. Pick up the controller.

And Press Start.

PART 4:
No Going Back

This part of the book hits different—not because everything's magically solved, but because you're not the same person you were at the start. You've put in the work. You've sat with the uncomfortable questions. You've gotten honest about the version of you that actually feels true.

Now? You're not starting from scratch anymore. You're starting from truth.

That means these next rules might sting a little more. They're bolder, sharper—no sugarcoating this time. You're ready for it.

But with that comes a choice: do you keep going, or do you retreat into something easier? It's tempting to go back to what's comfortable. To convince yourself you were being dramatic. That maybe you can keep peacekeeping your way through life. Or run away from the truth. Just enough to feel safe again.

You've carried a lot to get here—old habits, old fears, old stories about who you're allowed to be. They helped you survive, but they won't take you any further.

Because in these chapters you caught a glimpse of who you could be—and there's no unseeing it.

This is where you let go of the scripts that don't fit anymore. Where you stop explaining yourself to everyone who doesn't get it. Where you quiet the noise, trust your decisions, and move forward like someone who actually remembers what they're made of.

You don't have to prove anything anymore, but you do have to decide what you're going to do with all of this growth. Because the version of you who settled for almost? You already left them behind.

And from here?

There's no going back.

RULE #14:

Drop the Entitlement

Let's rip the Band-Aid off quickly: the world owes you absolutely nothing. Nada. Zip. And while that might feel a little harsh, it's also one of the most freeing truths you'll ever hear. Because once you accept that nothing is handed to you, you realize you're in control. Your life isn't a pre-written script, and you're not just waiting for your big break to come along. It's on you to make things happen—and honestly, that's the best part. You get to be the architect of your own story.

Here's the thing about entitlement: it's sneaky. It convinces you that you deserve success, recognition, or even help, just because. And when those things don't materialize? Cue the frustration and bitterness. But the hard truth is this: entitlement doesn't lead to happiness. It's like mashing buttons on a controller that's never been plugged in and wondering why nothing's happening.

When I was 22, I landed my first full-time office job. I was ready to embrace desk life, climb the corporate ladder, and prove myself as a leader. I started on the Help Desk, answering technical questions and resolving tickets for a web application. The system was simple: the more tickets you closed, the more money you made—and the higher your performance score.

So, I went all in. I studied the software inside and out, learning every corner of the system to maximize my efficiency. I became the go-to person for questions, not just from customers, but from my own team. And that's where things backfired.

I thought being the go-to expert would make me indispensable—that all the extra effort would pay off. But helping others meant my personal ticket count dropped, and despite being the most knowledgeable person on the team, my managers only saw the numbers. The promotional ladder was tied to metrics, not merit, and the person holding the power didn't see the full picture. I was frustrated. I waited for someone to recognize my value and hand me the promotion I "deserved." (What did I expect? A trophy for Most Overworked Employee?)

But no one did. And no one was going to.

Eventually, I realized that it was self-approval I lacked—and I was the one withholding it. So, I stopped waiting and started looking. I found an open position on another team, made the move, and now? I'm respected, I'm valued, and I'm making more money than ever. I found my own promotion.

If I had stayed stuck in self-pity, hoping someone else would fix things, I'd still be in that same role, miserable and overlooked. The world wasn't going to hand me a better situation. I had to go out and take it.

That's the thing: once I stopped waiting and took action, everything changed. And that shift in mindset? It applies to more than just jobs. It applies to every aspect of life.

Instead of assuming the world owes you, break out of the default. Start asking yourself: What can I earn? What can I contribute? Reframing your perspective from taking to contributing is a game-changer. It's the difference between waiting for a handout and building something you're genuinely proud of.

Effort doesn't always look good on Instagram. It's repetitive, inconvenient, and usually done in sweatpants. But it's what separates the people who actually build their dreams from the ones who aggressively manifest them while binging Netflix. Every time you put in the work—studying, practicing, showing up—you're leveling up. Success isn't magic. It's what happens when you show up, over and over again. Unless you were born into a billionaire family. In which case… congrats, I guess. This chapter isn't for you.

But effort isn't about hustling yourself into burnout. It's about working smarter. Set goals you can actually reach. Track your progress. Notice the progress you'd normally overlook. It's like an open-world game: you're not taking down the final boss on day one, but every side quest you finish gets you closer.

Let's talk about the role of a support system. Friends, family, mentors—they're your squad. But here's the catch: they're not obligated to carry you.

Picture this: you're getting ready to move and figure your friends will obviously show up because that's what friends do, right? You fire off a vague group text—"Hey, moving Saturday. Who's in?"—and sit back, confident they'll arrive with trucks and muscle.

But Saturday rolls around, and only one person shows up… in a Ford Focus. Now you're left dragging a sectional down the driveway, wondering where everybody went.

That's when it hits you: *Did I actually ask for help, or just expect it?*

It's totally okay to ask. But assuming others are required to help? That's where entitlement creeps in. Your friends don't owe you their Saturday, their truck, or their chiropractic bill. A better approach? Be specific. Plan ahead. Say, "Hey, I'd really appreciate your help this Saturday. If not, no worries—I've got a backup plan." That kind of clarity respects their time while proving you've taken responsibility for your own.

And when they do show up? Their help feels like the gift it is—not an obligation.

There's a sweet spot between doing everything alone and expecting everyone else to do it for you. Self-reliance means owning your role in your own life. Support means leaning on others when they're able and willing—and being the kind of person others can lean on, too. That's what builds trust and keeps relationships strong. No one likes feeling used, and no one wants to feel like they're burdening their friends.

A big part of that balance? Gratitude. When someone shows up for you—whether it's advice, a favor, or just listening—say thank you. Mean it. Write a note. Do the dishes. Return the favor when the time comes. It doesn't have to be big—just thoughtful.

But don't turn gratitude into scorekeeping. This isn't "I helped you move, so now you owe me tacos." It's not about settling debts. It's about building a relationship based on generosity, not transactions.

That same "you owe me" energy? It shows up in other places—like how we handle money, discounts, or free stuff.

Saving money is great. Who doesn't love a good deal or a free sample? But there's a line between being savvy and being, well… cringey. You know the type—the person who treats the free sample station like it's an all-you-can-eat buffet, or tries to haggle a $1 garage sale mug down to a quarter and then gets offended when it's declined.

Being thrifty? Great. Acting like generosity is owed to you? Not so much. Entitlement creeps in when you start treating someone else's generosity as an obligation—or act like you're owed more than what's being offered. Free samples, discounts, and low-priced items are acts of goodwill, not a challenge to see how much you can squeeze out of them.

Instead of obsessing over how much you can save, focus on the exchange itself. Did the garage sale owner already set fair prices? Cool—respect the effort they put into organizing it. Is the free sample at the grocery store just one bite? Perfect. Take it, thank the person handing it out, and move on without circling back five more times like it's a tasting menu.

Generosity isn't a buffet. Treating it like one doesn't just cheapen the moment—it devalues the gesture for everyone else, too.

There's a weird in-between phase no one warns you about—the part where life isn't falling apart, but it's not really moving forward either. You're technically okay. Bills are paid. Things are stable. But deep down, you're not growing. You're just coasting.

After I came home from my mission—early, unexpectedly, and not at all the way I thought it would go—I felt lost. Like I was back in familiar surroundings, but nothing felt familiar. I didn't know what was next, so I went back to what I knew. I picked up my old job at Target, same red shirt, same routines, like no time had passed.

I think part of me was hoping I could slip back into the version of myself I was before I left. The happy, grounded, life-on-track version. But he was gone—reshaped by what I'd just been through, and honestly, still grieving everything I thought that the mission was going to be.

So I coasted. Weeks turned into months. Months into longer. I told myself I was recovering, regrouping, taking a break. But at a certain point, I wasn't healing anymore—I was hiding. Waiting for clarity, motivation, some magical sign that it was time to move again. (Spoiler: that sign never came.)

What did come were those quiet, soul-splitting breakdowns—the kind where you're lying on your bed, staring at the ceiling, realizing how stuck you are. How much time you've let slip by. How much smaller your world has gotten while you kept pretending it was "fine."

I remember one night thinking, *Is this it?* Not in a throw-my-life-away kind of way. Just in that heavy, hollow sense of, *I thought I'd be further along by now.* I knew I wanted more—but wanting and doing are two very different muscles, and mine had atrophied from disuse.

Eventually, I did the only thing I could: I moved. I didn't have a master plan. But I updated my resume. I applied for a job I wasn't sure I could get. I forced myself to try.

I remember staring at the offer—equal parts overjoyed and panicked. Finally, a way out. A chance to move forward. I didn't know if it would be the right fit.

And yeah, that job came with its own frustrations. (You've already heard how that one played out.) But it was still a turning point—not because it was handed to me, but because I claimed it. I stopped waiting for a breakthrough and made one instead.

Maybe that's the real lesson. You don't need the perfect next step. You just need one that's yours.

The goal isn't comfort. It's growth, independence, and creating something you're proud of.

The world doesn't owe you success, happiness, or anything else—and that's okay, because that's not the bad news. It's the beginning of your new way of thinking.

The second you stop waiting for someone else to curate the perfect life for you, you realize: you're happier when you build it yourself. That's the power. That's the freedom.

The world owes you nothing—but you owe yourself everything.

Take stock of your relationships, your goals, and your mindset. Find one area where you've been leaning too hard on others—and take action. At the same time, ask yourself where you can give back. Generosity is a skill worth practicing.

Waiting won't change your life. Doing something will.

Make the call. Burn the excuse. Move.

No one is coming to save you.

Good. You'll do a better job anyway.

RULE #15:

Break the Loop

I spent years in emotional triage. Home wasn't just home—it was a battlefield. Tension buzzed under the surface like a flickering fluorescent light you couldn't quite locate. You don't notice it at first. Not really. You just start walking softer, talking quieter, bracing for the crack you know is coming but can't predict. It becomes second nature. Normal, even.

So I became the buffer. The bridge. The fixer.

If there was silence, I filled it. If there was anger, I diffused it. I kept the peace—not because anyone asked me to, but because I couldn't stand the alternative. It felt like survival. Like if I could keep everyone else okay, maybe I'd be okay too.

It took me years to realize how much of myself I'd left behind in the process.

At first, it looked like care. It looked like love. I was the good kid, the sensitive one, the "mature for my age" emotional translator who could see everyone's side and play therapist. But over time, that role stopped being a skill and started becoming a trap. I didn't know who I was outside of it. I couldn't tell the difference between being helpful and being needed. I mistook managing other people's emotions for being valuable. And yeah—I got really good at putting out fires. Just never my own.

I wish I could say there was some dramatic breaking point—one big explosion that snapped it all into place. But the truth was quieter than that. More exhausting than explosive. I just started noticing how tired I always was. How tight my chest felt. How I'd walk into a room already scanning for tension, already bracing to become whatever version of myself the moment required.

I started to wonder—what would happen if I just… didn't?

So I tested it. I let a conversation trail off instead of rescuing it. I let people sit in their discomfort. I stopped filling every silence with reassurance. I stopped treating their chaos like it was my job to manage.

And you know what happened?

Nothing.

Nothing blew up. No one fell apart. The world didn't end. It just kept spinning. And for the first time, I wasn't spinning with it. I was still. I was—strangely—free.

I'd been so afraid that if I stopped holding everything together, it would all collapse. But it turned out I was just one person. I always had been. And the weight I'd been carrying? Most of it wasn't even mine.

That was the deep end. But these patterns don't just show up in big, dramatic ways—they sneak into the little stuff, too. The everyday annoyances. The low-stakes spiral you've almost stopped noticing.

Like when you complain about your job every single day but never update your résumé. Or when your friend flakes again and you're annoyed, but you say "no worries!" for the fifth time this month. Or when you glare at the pile of laundry while bingeing a show *about* productivity.

We all do it. We all sit in situations that frustrate us—not because we love the frustration, but because complaining about it feels easier than facing what it would actually take to change it.

Complaining without action doesn't move you forward. It just keeps you stuck.

And don't get me wrong—venting can be good. Healthy, even. It clears out emotional congestion. It helps you process, reflect, maybe even laugh a little before moving on.

But complaining is different. Complaining loops. It circles the drain. It spirals into frustration theater. It tricks you into thinking you're solving the problem when really, you're just narrating it. Again. And again.

And again.

Here's where things shift.

What if every complaint was actually a decision point?

Can I fix this? Can I let it go? Or am I just looping it because letting go would mean it's really over?

That's the fork in the road. That's where change starts—not with a breakthrough, but with a choice.

If you want to break the loop, you have to make a choice. Fix it. Release it. But don't keep circling.

And yet—we hesitate. We stall. We convince ourselves we need more time, more clarity, more proof.

We wait for things to magically improve. For a boss to finally notice our effort. For a partner to read our mind. For a messy room to clean itself. (Okay, maybe not that one. But still.) We act like staying in limbo is neutral—like it's safer than doing something. But it's not. It's draining. It eats up your energy, your focus, your time—things you don't get back.

And maybe the worst part? It robs you of your agency. Because being stuck isn't a personality trait. It's not who you are.

It's just a moment you haven't moved through yet.

Not every situation requires a life overhaul. Sometimes, it's just about doing the thing instead of spiraling around it.

Like this: One week, I kept complaining about how cluttered my bedroom was and how it was stressing me out. Every time I walked in, I'd sigh dramatically. I joked about how "I was living in chaos." I even sent a friend a picture with a caption like, "Send thoughts and prayers."

And then one afternoon, I finally did something about it. I put on a playlist, set a timer for 20 minutes, and got to work. And the part that annoyed me most? It wasn't even that bad. I'd spent more energy *complaining* about the mess than it took to clean it up.

Sometimes the problem isn't actually the problem. It's the hesitation. The overthinking. The dread. The way your brain turns a ten-minute task into a whole existential crisis.

Of course, not everything can be cleaned up with a playlist and a 20-minute timer.

That's when fixing it stops being an option—and starts becoming a weight. You try, and try, and try again. And it still hurts. Nothing shifts. Nothing heals. Not really. You reach a point where the only way forward… is through. Without it.

That's when the other half of this rule kicks in.

Move. On. Already.

And just to be clear—moving on doesn't mean forgetting. Or pretending it didn't matter. Or acting like you're fine when you're not.

It means protecting your peace. It means saying, "This doesn't get to own me anymore."

It might mean ending a relationship you thought would last forever. Or letting go of the life you imagined you'd be living by now. Or finally accepting that someone won't change—no matter how badly you want them to.

It might mean grieving something you never got. Closure. Recognition. A real apology.

You won't always get what you deserve. But you don't have to let the lack of it define you.

Here's the hard truth: some people will never give you the closure, respect, or awareness you deserve. And if you're not careful, you'll waste years screaming into a void, hoping they'll wake up and care.

I've been there. When my best friend walked away without a conversation, without a reason—just gone—it gutted me. I held onto that silence like it was something I could eventually fix. I kept replaying what I'd said, what I hadn't said, trying to solve a puzzle she'd already walked away from.

I've spent nights crafting perfect comebacks I'll never say out loud. I've carried someone else's indifference like it was mine to fix. And one day, it hit me—*why am I giving so much of my life to someone who isn't even thinking about me?*

You don't owe your energy to people who wouldn't notice if you went silent.

You can't control how others treat you. But you *can* control how long you let them live rent-free in your head. And the longer they stay, the less space you have for the people who actually show up.

So stop replaying the tape. Stop keeping them alive in your head like they still have a say. You've already lost enough sleep.

Some people aren't worth fixing. They aren't even worth forgetting. They're just… irrelevant.

And that's okay. Because the second you stop giving them power, you get it back.

Life's too short to waste on resentment, or what-ifs, or people who couldn't bother to stay. The real power is in choosing where your energy goes next.

And if you're not sure where to start? That's okay. Sometimes I'm not either.

Here's a reflection I come back to when I feel myself spiraling: 1. Name it — What exactly am I upset about? Not just the surface-level "they were rude," but the deeper need underneath. 2. Claim it — Why does it matter to me? What wound is this poking at? 3. Frame it — What's actually in my control right now? 4. Release it — Can I do something about it? If not, what would it look like to let it go?

Then—breathe. Repeat if you need to. Take a walk. Delete the text draft. Journal it out. Cry in your car. Whatever helps get it out of your body.

Then move. Even if it's just one inch forward. Even if it's just deciding not to stew in it for the rest of the day. That still counts.

You want to know why this rule really matters?

Because your time is limited. Your peace is sacred. And every ounce of energy you waste on things you won't change—or can't—is energy you're not spending on what actually matters.

Like healing. Or laughing. Or building something better than the bad hand you were dealt.

I think about all the things I missed while I was busy managing everyone else's problems. How many times I stayed behind to mediate instead of going out with friends. How often I kept my phone on, "just in case." How many times I said "I'm fine" when I wasn't, because telling the truth felt like more work than swallowing it.

You don't always notice the cost in the moment. It sneaks up later—when you realize how many relationships you didn't nurture, how much rest you didn't take, how often you post-poned your own joy. It shows up when you finally sit still... and realize you're not even sure who you are outside of every-one else's crisis.

That's the real danger of not moving on. It doesn't just keep you stuck—it makes you forget what forward even feels like.

This isn't about being cold. It's about being clear. It's about finally telling the truth:

That carrying everyone else's burdens didn't save you. That complaining didn't fix it. That staying stuck didn't keep you safe. And that letting go—scary and uncomfortable as it was—was the only thing that actually gave you your life back.

I remember the moment. I was driving, windows down, blasting music—and I realized I wasn't holding my breath anymore.

I hadn't even noticed I'd been doing it, but suddenly… it was gone. The weight. The tension. The constant low hum of responsibility I'd gotten used to carrying like background noise.

I didn't have all the answers. I wasn't "healed." But I was lighter. And for the first time in forever, it felt like the air around me actually belonged to me.

You already know what it is.

The thing you keep circling. The story you've worn out. The frustration you could recite in your sleep.

Maybe it's something you vent about every other week. Maybe it's a conversation you've rewritten a dozen times in your head, hoping for a better ending. Or maybe it's quieter than that—just a low-grade ache you've carried so long, it feels like part of you now.

Whatever it is, the question still stands: are you going to do something about it?

Fix it if you can. Release it if you can't. And if you're not ready to do either, at least be honest about how much it's costing you to carry it.

You don't need a perfect plan. You just need one true step in a new direction.

Because staying stuck is a choice, too.

And you?

You've got better places to be.

RULE #16:

Simplify to Amplify

Modern life is a masterclass in overcomplication. From apps promising to optimize every second of your day to closets packed with clothes that still leave you saying, "I have nothing to wear," it's easy to lose sight of what actually matters.

We hoard things, overcommit, hold onto habits that don't serve us, and leave way too many tabs open in Chrome. Then we wonder why we feel so overwhelmed.

I used to think I was good at multitasking—until I realized I was just bad at focusing on anything. Turns out, being busy and being effective aren't the same thing.

You ever look around your space and realize it feels… loud? Not in words—just in vibes. Like, somehow the mess on your desk is shouting at you? Clutter—physical or mental—takes up more than just space. It crowds your confidence and drowns out your priorities. It weighs on you, distracts you, and turns even simple tasks into uphill battles.

Somewhere between "answering emails" and "rearranging the apps on my phone for no reason," I convince myself I'm being productive. I call it efficiency. My to-do list calls it denial. Meanwhile, the actual priorities sit there, judging me—just like that stack of unread books I swore I'd get through.

Look, I engage in retail therapy too sometimes. But I promise you don't need more stuff. You need fewer distractions.

This is why we're always exhausted. We're drowning in things we don't need, filling our calendars with obligations we don't even like, and leaving zero room to actually breathe.

That's the weight of overabundance. It doesn't crash through the door—it sneaks in quietly, wrapped in good intentions and shiny opportunities, whispering, "You can handle one more thing." And maybe you can. But that's how you end up car-rying a life full of stuff, commitments, and expectations that don't even feel like yours.

It's like overpacking for a trip and dragging around a giant suit-case that could've been a carry-on. You're sweating through the airport, shuffling past everyone, wondering why you brought three jackets to the beach—and realizing, too late, that none of them match anything anyway .

At first, it feels like responsibility. Like "adulting." But over time, the line blurs between what actually matters to you and what you've picked up out of habit, guilt, or expectation.

All that excess quiets your instincts, dulls your spark, and leaves you weirdly disconnected from the parts of yourself that used to feel sharp and alive. It doesn't just take up space—it takes up *you*.

Life doesn't have to feel this heavy.

Clearing out the excess—physically and mentally—isn't just about tidying up. It's how you get your focus back. Your energy back. Your *life* back.

This rule isn't a lecture on decluttering your closet (though we'll get to that). It's about adopting a mindset that values clarity over chaos, intentionality over impulse, and focus over frenzy. Simplifying your life—your space, your time, your habits—isn't about deprivation. It's about freedom. The kind that lets you do whatever you want, thrive instead of survive, and dream big while staying grounded in the present.

Right now, stop reading and take a look around your living space. Did you look yet? Chances are, it's filled with things you thought you'd need, love, or use all the time. And yet… that drone you bought on a whim or your once-cherished Funko Pop collection isn't exactly sparking joy anymore.

Every item you own demands something from you: a corner of your space, a sliver of your attention, a few seconds of your time. The more you own, the more those demands pile up.

Now imagine walking into a room where everything has a purpose. No clutter, no chaos, just the essentials. There's a kind of peace that comes from being surrounded by only what serves you. That's the power of simplicity.

I'm not saying you need to ditch everything and live out of a backpack (unless that's your vibe). But what if you let yourself release the excess—no justification needed? That shelf of unread books, the drawer full of random cords, the decorative knick-knacks you haven't noticed since 2020… what would it feel like to let them go?

Decluttering should mean *getting rid* of things, but somehow it always turns into a complicated game of Tetris where everything stays, just in slightly different places. My first instinct when decluttering? Buying more storage bins. Because *obviously*, the problem isn't that I own too much—it's that I haven't invested in enough overpriced plastic rectangles to hide it in. Problem solved, right?

Let me tell you about the time I decided to tackle my closet. At first, I thought, "How hard can it be?" Thirty minutes in, I was knee-deep in clothes I hadn't worn in years, wondering why I still owned things that haven't fit me since high school. Some still had tags on. Some I kept because they reminded me of someone else's opinion of me—who I thought I was supposed to be.

That's when it hit me. I wasn't just decluttering clothes—I was untangling versions of myself I'd held onto out of fear. Fear of losing my identity. Fear of needing those pieces again. Fear of not being enough without them.

The process wasn't cute (I may have cried a little), but when I finished, something shifted. Suddenly, picking out an outfit was easy. I didn't have to sift through items I didn't even like. My room felt lighter—and honestly, *so did I.*

Because simplifying wasn't just about clearing space. It was about letting go of a version of myself I didn't need anymore.

You're not here to shrink into yesterday's version of yourself.

You don't have to tackle your whole house at once. Zero in on something manageable—one drawer, one shelf, one category. Be ruthless about what stays. Ask yourself: "Do I use it? Do I love it? Does it add value to my life?" If not, from the mouth of Marie Kondo's translator, "thank it for its service and let it go." Arigatō, sayōnara. Donate, recycle, or toss—just don't let it linger.

Minimalism isn't just about physical stuff though. Your schedule can be just as overwhelming as your junk drawer: packed, chaotic, and somehow full of things you don't even remember agreeing to. Think about how many commitments you've made out of guilt or presumed obligation. Are all of them really worth your time?

It's okay to say no. In fact, it's liberating. Every time you decline an unnecessary meeting or skip an event you're not excited about, you're saying yes to something more important: your own priorities. I'm not saying you should ghost every social event to stay home and play Xbox (I'm also not *not* saying that).

Simplifying your schedule doesn't mean doing nothing or never going out with your friends. It means doing what matters most, and recognizing when your body and mind need a break from the noise.

One way to start is by taking inventory of your time. Write down everything you're committed to over the next week. Then ask yourself: "Which of these things truly aligns with my goals and values?" Cut what doesn't. It's easy to assume that being busy means being productive, but real progress comes from focusing on what actually matters. Make room for rest, creativity, and the things that light you up—and know you don't need a reason to deserve it.

The right friends won't get mad if you occasionally need to prioritize other things. And honestly, you don't owe anyone an explanation or excuse for why you're focusing on yourself.

When it comes to work, finding balance in your schedule is critical in avoiding burnout. In my job, meetings often get scheduled for me, and my calendar is either packed to the brim or eerily empty; there's rarely an in-between. Some weeks, I'd be juggling back-to-back meetings, barely finding time to breathe. Other weeks? Crickets. The whiplash was real—and exhausting.

Eventually, I had a conversation with the people scheduling those meetings and brought up the idea of spreading them out when possible. It made no sense for me to be burnt out one week and bored out of my mind the next.

As you'd expect, they listened and agreed, but failed to fix the issue in practice. Instead, I started blocking out small windows of time on my calendar to force them to spread out my meetings around those blocks.

Taking that step made an immediate difference. Instead of drowning one week and drifting the next, I finally found my stride—and it made everything feel a little more human.

Now, let's talk about your phone. When was the last time you opened your phone and actually felt better afterward?

How many unread emails, unused apps, and endless notifications are stealing your focus and wrecking your perfect home screen aesthetic?

Digital clutter might not take up physical space, but it can be just as (if not more) exhausting. Every notification is a tiny interruption, pulling you out of the moment and back into the vortex.

Clear the junk. Delete the apps you haven't opened in months. Unsubscribe from the emails you never read. Turn off the notifications you don't need.

Treat your phone like a digital closet—only keep what you actually use.

Take it a step further with Focus Mode. Customize it for work, relaxation, or sleep so only the most essential notifications break through. This one tweak can seriously reduce distractions and help you reclaim your brainpower.

And if you're feeling bold? Try a digital detox. A full day—or even just a few hours—unplugged. No scrolling, no buzzing, no background hum of everyone else's opinions. You'll be surprised how quiet your mind becomes when it doesn't have to compete with a screen.

One of the clearest memories I have of this came during my senior year of all-state choir in high school. Two hundred of us, no phones—just music. Every note demanded presence. Every breath was shared. I remember feeling completely immersed—physically, emotionally, spiritually. It wasn't about doing more. It was about being fully there.

And that's what simplifying gives you back: the ability to actually live where you are.

Living a lifestyle that reduces physical clutter doesn't just free up space—it reshapes the way you think. It sharpens your instincts. It helps you move through life with less friction and more intention.

When you're faced with a decision, it's easy to spiral. But your choices don't need to be perfect—they just need to reflect your values.

Ask yourself: Does this align with what actually matters to you? Does it support the life you're building? Do you want it—or are you just used to it?

That's the real power of simplifying—not just in your space, but in your mind. It clears the fog so you can move with purpose, not pressure.

And no, this isn't just about your closet or your phone. It's about letting go of the distractions, expectations, and outdated narratives that are cluttering your sense of self.

Sometimes we hold onto clutter—physical or emotional—because it makes us feel useful. Busy. Safe. But busyness is not the same as purpose. And peace is not the same as passivity.

Choosing simplicity is a power move in a world that feeds on your overwhelm. It's not about less for the sake of minimalism. It's about less of what doesn't matter, so there's more room for what does.

This week, pick one area of your life to simplify—not to impress anyone, but to reconnect with who you actually are.

Ask yourself: What have I outgrown? What no longer feels like me? What's weighing me down that I never meant to carry?

Let it go. Not because it's trendy. Because it's time.

And when you finally stop letting clutter define your life, you'll wonder why you ever let it take up so much space.

Because you're not just cleaning house.

You're clearing the path for who you're becoming.

RULE #17:

Throw Out the Rule Book

Rules exist for a reason. They keep traffic flowing, help us live together without descending into chaos, and ensure the barista doesn't make your latte with motor oil. (Unless it's an artisanal blend—then that'll be $9.75.)

This rule is about learning when to follow those rules, and when to, hypothetically (or literally) throw out the rule book altogether. And just to be clear: when I say "Throw Out the Rule Book," I don't mean *this* one. I'm talking about society's version—the checklist of what your life should look like, full of expectations you never actually agreed to.

Not all rules are created equal—some help us thrive, others are outdated, and a few never made sense to begin with.

What do you do when the rules start to feel more like shackles than scaffolding? You challenge them.

Society loves rules. Some are unspoken, like "Don't cut in line," "Don't talk during a movie," or "The middle urinal doesn't actually exist." Others are more rigid, like career expectations or the timeline for major life milestones. Go to school, get a job, buy a house, get married, have kids, retire—you know the drill. It's a script. And for some people, it works perfectly.

But what if it doesn't work for you?

Living unapologetically means stepping outside of society's expectations and pursuing what genuinely brings you joy, even if it means breaking tradition.

Maybe you don't want the house with the white picket fence. Maybe you want to travel the world, start a nonprofit, or work as a freelance artist. Society's rules might whisper, "That's not practical," but practicality is subjective. What's impractical to them might be the only thing keeping you alive.

When I was younger, I often felt boxed in by expectations—not just from society, but from myself. I thought success had to look a certain way: graduating from high school, going on a mission trip for the church, getting married and starting a family, buying a new house and a car, hitting all the markers of a "respectable" life.

But the truth is, those markers made me feel like a prisoner in my own life—and didn't bring me the joy I was promised.

Still, I tried to want the "normal" life. I told myself I just needed to push through—that maybe if I checked a few more boxes, the joy would finally kick in. I'd watch other people hit the same milestones and feel this strange mix of admiration and confusion, like... *am I broken for not feeling what they're feeling?*

Eventually, I stopped forcing it.

What actually brought relief? Small acts of rebellion against the script.

Like not going back to church right away after my mission, even though I didn't have the language yet for why it didn't feel right. Like living at home when I was supposed to be "moving forward," and deciding that financial stability mattered more than appearances. Like working retail longer than I meant to—not because I lacked ambition, but because I needed space to breathe and figure out who I was without all the pressure.

Tiny decisions, on paper. But each time I stepped away from the "life checklist", I realized it wasn't protecting me—it was the thing standing between me and the life I actually wanted.

Challenging the rules isn't as easy as flipping a switch. It's disorienting. It's exposing. It's standing in front of people who have known you forever and realizing you're about to disappoint them. It's feeling like you have to justify every choice, defend every deviation, and constantly prove you're not just making a mistake.

Maybe the nay-sayers are right. Maybe the script is safer.

But what about the other side? The second you stop waiting for approval. The weight that lifts when you realize you don't owe anyone an explanation for living your life in a way that makes sense to you. The quiet confidence that comes when you choose your own path, not because it's expected, but because it's yours. At first, rewriting the rules feels like rebellion. Eventually, it just feels like coming home.

Questioning the status quo doesn't mean rejecting everything outright. For me, it started with a pause long enough to ask, "Does this make sense for me?" and "Am I living my truth?" If the answer was no, it wasn't a crisis—it was a cue to rethink and recalibrate.

Because if you're not asking those questions, you'll find yourself living a life built on someone else's values, not your own.

Finding the courage to walk away from pieces of your life that don't feel right is a massive step toward inner peace. But here's the catch: it's not just about the decision. It's about standing by it when the world pushes back.

It'll feel uncomfortable. Maybe even painful. I know from experience. But that discomfort fades. And when it does, what's left is a kind of quiet pride—a certainty that lets you look back and say, "That was the moment I found my unapologetic self."

I know firsthand how hard it is to step off the expected path, because when I did, it felt like the whole world was watching. When I left my church mission, I knew it was the right decision. I knew I wasn't abandoning anything; I was choosing myself, my well-being, and my future. But that didn't stop the shame. The whispers, the judgment, the constant feeling that I had somehow failed at something I shouldn't have done at all.

At first, I tried to explain myself. I wanted people to understand that I wasn't lost, I was finally finding my truth. But the more I justified, the more I realized I didn't need to. Their rule book wasn't mine to follow. The instant I stopped trying to make it make sense, their expectations started to lift.

Walking away from something that doesn't serve you is one thing. Learning to live with the consequences, both internal and external, is another. Challenging the rules isn't always met with applause. Sometimes, it's met with silence. Other times, it's met with resistance. But every time, it's met with clarity. And that clarity? It's worth everything.

Challenging the rules doesn't mean constant rebellion. It means paying attention. It means staying curious enough to ask why before you obey.

If you're going to follow a rule, know *why*. Blind obedience might look responsible, but it's not the same as living with integrity. When you understand the reason behind a rule, you get to decide—on purpose—whether it still belongs. Until then, the rule is making the decision for you. And that's not agency. That's autopilot.

Not every rule deserves your obedience. And not every choice needs a defense. You're allowed to live in alignment without putting your life on trial.

I used to think I had to explain every decision that went against the grain—especially when it made people uncomfortable. I overexplained, overjustified, overapologized. But that's the trap:

once you start believing you owe everyone an explanation, you never stop performing. You don't need to apologize for living a life that makes sense to you. Save your "sorrys" for when they matter. For everything else, confidence will do.

Rethinking the rules doesn't mean tossing them out or pretending they never mattered. Some rules exist to protect people. Those deserve respect—even when they're inconvenient.

Others are more cultural than moral—shaped by context, custom, or someone else's comfort level. Those are the ones you get to bend, question, or discard when they stop reflecting who you are.

When you challenge the status quo, lead with empathy. Just because you've outgrown a way of thinking doesn't mean everyone else has. People evolve at their own pace. Their path is theirs. Yours is yours. Being a rebel doesn't mean being a jerk.

This rule is about ownership—choosing your life, not just reacting to it.

You don't have to accept every rule you were handed—especially the ones built for someone else's version of success. You can pause. You can question. You can rewrite.

I used to think I had to be the "good kid" to be a good person. The one who followed the rules, kept the peace, made everyone proud. But being good isn't the same as being perfect—and it's definitely not the same as being obedient. I'm still kind. I still care. But I've stopped trying to be the perfect baby version of myself who never messes up, never pushes back, and never makes anyone uncomfortable.

I make mistakes on purpose now. I disappoint people. I choose things they don't understand—sometimes while they're judging me to my face. But I own my choices. And honestly? That's what good-ness looks like to me now: not being flawless, but being free.

Maybe that's the ultimate plot twist: the only rule that ever really mattered was giving yourself permission to break the rest.

I've spent years trying to get it right. Trying to be palatable. Predictable. Polished. But no performance—no matter how convincing—can give you the peace that comes from choosing your life with both hands.

It takes time to build that kind of trust with yourself. To listen. To believe what you hear. But once you do, the need for approval starts to shrink—and your life starts to sound like your own.

So when a society's arbitrary or contradictory rules no longer fit who you're becoming? Throw them out. Then stand a little taller.

Not because you broke them.

But because you made your own.

CONCLUSION

As we reach the end, thank you for coming along on this ride. Writing this book has been equal parts exhilarating and humbling, and knowing that you've stuck with me—even through the questionable anecdotes and frequent tangents—means the world.

Whether you laughed, cringed, or rolled your eyes, I hope you found something valuable here. (And if you did all three in one chapter? Honestly—same.)

But this isn't just about what you've read.

It's about what you do next.

Everything before this was an invitation. A challenge. A call to action.

Maybe you've realized it's time to take control. To break free from the rules that no longer serve you. To stop living like you're waiting for a permission slip.

Maybe you've decided to embrace joy in the smallest moments—laughing at your own mistakes, savoring a quiet cup of hot chocolate, or finally muting that one group chat that's just endless memes.

Regardless, the shift has already started. You're not stuck. You're stepping into something bigger.

You don't have to get it perfect. Just get it honest. That first wobbly baby step? It still moves you forward.

You're not just a participant in your own life—you're the author. You hold the pen. No one else gets to write the ending.

Whether it's cutting out distractions, speaking your truth, or finally simplifying the chaos—your choices shape your world.

Yes, life will throw plot twists. Yes, some rules will need rewriting. But you? You're not powerless. You're adaptable, relentless, and entirely capable of creating a life that actually feels like yours.

These rules aren't here to restrict you. They're reminders—gentle nudges pointing you back to what matters. Guidelines, not guardrails. Tools, not commandments.

They're not sacred. They're not permanent. They're meant to evolve with you.

Let them guide you when you need direction. Let them go when you don't. Your life was never meant to fit inside someone else's blueprint. The goal isn't to follow perfectly—it's to live honestly.

So take what resonates, leave what doesn't, and trust yourself to know the difference.

Because it was never about following the rules. It was about remembering that you get to write your own.

These were your training wheels. Now? You get to decide if it's time to ride full speed ahead.

Here's your challenge (not homework—challenges are more fun, right?): pick one or two rules that stuck with you. Maybe it's committing to honesty, living with intention, or simplifying the chaos in your life. Maybe it's ditching comparison or being the hero of your own story. Maybe it's learning to balance ambition with presence, dreaming big while cherishing what you already have.

Whatever it is, start there. Notice how it shows up in your life. Try things. If it clicks, great. If not? Rework it. That's the power you hold.

If there's one rule to carry with you, let it be this: Be unapologetically you. These pages were only the beginning. You get to decide how the rest unfolds. Own who you are. Break what never fit. Build something so honest and so bold that no one could ever mistake it for anyone else's.

As we close this chapter—and this book—I want to thank you once more. Thank you for showing up. For reflecting. For being willing to question, to rethink, to grow. Writing these words has been a privilege, but it's your journey that gives them meaning.

These rules are here to help you thrive, not box you in. They aren't gospel—they're guideposts. Use what helps. Leave what doesn't. Evolve them as you evolve.

Because these were my truths—but the story that matters now is the one only you can tell.

So make it real. Make it yours.

And make it unforgettable.

Unapologetically,

Elijah Bottomley

ABOUT THE AUTHOR

Elijah Bottomley wrote UNAPOLOGETIC: The (Un)Rule Book as something who spends a lot of time noticing what people say, what they mean, and what gets lost in between.

He tends to think deeply about tone, timing, and impact. He cares how things land, even when that care doesn't always read the way he intends. He's selective with his energy, deeply loyal once trust is earned, and more interested in honesty than being impressive.

This book grew from a deep desire to help others discover the freedom that comes from living unapologetically. It reflects how Elijah chooses to live in the world—paying attention, choosing deliberately, radiating positivity, and trying to be real without performing for approval.

www.ingramcontent.com/pod-product-compliance
Lightning Source LLC
Chambersburg PA
CBHW051621120626
46551CB00014B/1887
* 9 7 9 8 9 9 9 3 9 4 0 1 9 *